The *Candour* A.B.C of Politics

The *Candour* A.B.C. of Politics

By

Rosine de Bounevialle

The A.K. Chesterton Trust

2016

Printed and published in 2016. First Edition.

© **The A.K. Chesterton Trust**, BM Candour, London, WC1N 3XX, UK.

Website: www.candour.org.uk

ISBN: 978-0-9932885-7-9

If you knew the gift of God
and what Heaven is.
If you could hear the angels singing
and see me among them...
If, only for an instant, you could contemplate,
just like me,
the Beauty before which all beauties turn pale.
Trust me.
When the day, which god has stated and knows, arrives
and your soul, which has been preceded by mine,
enters this Heaven,
That day you will see me again,
you will feel that I still love you,
that I have always loved you
and you will find my heart
with all its love purified.

You will see me in transfiguration,
in an ecstasy of happiness.
No longer waiting for death,
but walking with you
and holding your hand along new paths of light and life.

So, wipe your tears away
and don't cry, if you love me...

St. Augustin

Rosine de Bounevialle in 1992

CONTENTS

Foreword

The *Candour* A.B.C. of Politics was originally serialised in *Candour* between August 1989 and August 1995. It was intended to publish in book form the text that Rosine de Bounevialle referred to as her "only literary baby" long ago, but it was not to be in her lifetime.

The enclosed articles are an idiosyncratic and wonderful testament of her values. One hundred years after her birth it is fitting that such an influential and elemental force be remembered and recognised. Rosine has been very much underestimated, she was never interested in political frippery, and although tiny in frame had the heart of a British lioness. Quick to protect her people, those she loved, and dangerous when it came to dealing with those who traduced them.

We have also included some of Rosine's autobiographical articles entitled "However Did It Happen to Me" and some photographs. Thank you to Jeff Carson and Tregunta Cathcart for proof reading.

Not everyone will be fortunate enough to meet a Rosine de Bounevialle in their time. This book is a small thank you.

Rosine Maria de Bounevialle, 1916 - 1999.

Present!

Rob Black

The A.K. Chesterton Trust
December 2016

An Introduction

By Colin Todd

We have left it late, about twenty years late, to finally publish what Miss Rosine Maria de Bounevialle called "my only literary baby" *The Candour A.B.C. of Politics*. I had so wanted Rosine to hold a copy. (And help me with this Foreword!). It is important that this work appears now in the 100th anniversary year of Rosine's birth in 1916.

I first subscribed to *Candour* when I was fourteen after seeing a small advertisement in an issue of John Tyndall's journal *Spearhead* in 1976, then in support of the National Front.

I envy people who say they have no regrets in life although I think it shows a lack of imagination. From 1979 I was in the Royal Navy and based in Portsmouth and I would regularly travel on the London to Pompey rail route and past Liss station. If I had had the wit to look it up in a road map I would have discovered that is the next village from Liss Forest. This being the home of Miss Rosine de Bounevialle and *Candour*. I could have met Rosine years earlier than I did and much could be very different.

Finally I made it to Forest House in the late 1980's. Oddly enough that was in the company of Nick Griffin. Mr. Griffin was there to put forward one of his many money making 'schemes'. Which have at least twice ended in bankruptcy. He wanted Rosine to let him run a paint ball business on her land. He was cut down in short time. "If you think I am going to have people running around here in uniforms with guns you must be mad" was the gist. I had nothing to say apart from hello and goodbye that time. Later, after I had moved into Forest House as a guest and general factotum, Rosine confided to me that at that first meeting she had thought to herself "He is the one!" meaning that she saw me as her successor. Pure intuition.

Rosine with her mother, Cecilia, father, Alec and brother, the magnificently named Casimir Marmeduke de Bounevialle DFC (RAF) moved to Forest House in 1947. Born and raised in Croydon when it was still a leafy suburb the family moved to a house called Beaumont Lodge at Ilfield Wood in Sussex.

There an eighteen year old Rosine became great pals with an old rogue and neighbour called Robert Standish Sievier. They would go to the nearest picture houses often and races where Rosine became an aficionado of the Turf. Bob Sievier was once a multi-millionaire and racehorse owner who had been a soldier, boxer, actor, bookmaker, professional gambler and publisher of the Winning Post. His horse Sceptre won four of the five English classic races in 1902. Rosine's father Alec was an inventor "of genius" who left business and the running of the family to his wife Cecilia. It was she who moved the family to a bungalow called the Skep at Rake off the historic old London Portsmouth Road, now the A3, during the phoney war in 1939.

During the war Rosine worked as a telephonist at the Admiralty in London and after the war spent time as the stewardess on her brothers one plane (a DC3) airline mainly ferrying oil workers around the Middle East. Until that came to an end when the aircraft was written off having crashed on landing at Jerusalem. (No casualties apparently).

Then a spell at the hated United Nations HQ in New York where her best friend Lalya, a Yugoslav girl Rosine had met in London during the war also worked.

On returning to Hampshire and Forest House Rosine became involved with the Liss Young Conservatives, but her disgust at the Suez disaster in 1956 and the capitulation of the British Government in the face of U.S. pressure led to a break. If I remember correctly at about this time Rosine had met a British army officer on a train and chatting together they had got on to politics. That officer happened to have a couple of issues of *Candour* (founded 1953) in his briefcase which he handed to Rosine. That changed her life forever. For better or worse.

First Rosine made enquiries and visited the *Candour* office in London. This, of course was also the office for the League of Empire Loyalists (founded 1954). Well. That was that. Next Rosine led the whole of the Liss Young Conservatives into the LEL[1]. Something the Tories around here never forgot or forgave. Not that Rosine gave a fig!

While Rosine lived, Forest House was a wonderful place full of people and laughter. Another of my regrets is that during the long winter evenings when Rosine would reminisce about her life and especially her days of excitement in the League of Empire Loyalists I did not have a tape recorder on constant duty. For all that the lady was tiny she had the heart of a lioness and I was sure there would always be more time.

Because Rosine had an 'open door' policy throughout warmer weather people would simply walk into the house and call at the study where Rosine would usually be found at her large desk. Overflowing with papers, books and the black and white tomcat Aeneas snoring gently away. As Rosine would say when searching high and low for that missing vital letter, bill or order "always under the bloody cat".

One time three middle aged men climbed out of a car in the drive way walked quietly past me and parked themselves in the study where Rosine had her desk facing the window and with her back to the door.

---

[1] If you do not already have a copy you need to order from us *The History of the League of Empire Loyalists and Candour* by Hugh Mc Neile and Rob Black for more information.

I went upstairs and could hear the sound of chatter and teacups soon after. After an hour Rosine came looking for me and wanted to know why I was not entertaining my guests. "Rosine I have never seen them before. I thought they were your friends". "Oh Colin darling I have no idea who they are either." Between us it took half an hour of gently working the conversation before we learned that they were three very peculiar odd bods who been in the National Front in the seventies, had been given Rosine's address by yet another person we had never heard of, and had not thought to introduce themselves apparently under the impression that they were evidently nationalists of such standing and importance that it was not necessary. They left after boring us with their thoughts on "the only way forward is" line having drunk the tea eaten the cake and biscuits and leaving not a penny for *Candour* and declining to even take a free copy. A wasted afternoon but it gave us a laugh many times later.

Memories of Rosine

My first visit to Forest House was for a meeting with friends. I remember the atmosphere, the welcome. I did not know Rosine, or who she was at all.

We had a long walk altogether in the forest and I had an accident with some old barbed wire. I cut my leg and Rosine and Colin took care of me at once. I have the scar to remind me of my first visit. During my subsequent visits I discovered a great lady. Evening discussions by the open fire in the study. Rosine and a neighbour Robert taught me how to play backgammon. Rosine let me drive her car in the countryside while I was preparing for my driving licence exam. Colin in the back seat was always so scared.

I loved her library. Full of marvellous books. Her desk was always invaded by masses of papers and Aeneas the cat that was wished on her. She gave me books which I keep preciously.

She was generous. There was always room for someone. She made me feel like a special guest. I remember a crazy spring cleaning session when we were beating the study's rugs with a cricket bat at the back of the house. She was exhausted but still lively. When we relaxed we drank sherry in the gardens or on the settee in the study.

She was beautiful and elegant. Physically and spiritually. Dynamic, strong, straight and devoted to her ideals. Devoted to her friends. To Colin whom she loved like her son.

Marie-Isabelle

Paris, 2016

INTRODUCTION TO THE *CANDOUR* A.B.C. OF POLITICS

by ROSINE DE BOUNEVIALLE

THIS is to introduce the *Candour* A.B.C. of politics, which will appear in subsequent issues. But first it is necessary to know what we mean by 'politics' in this context.

Most of us under fifty years old have been taught and trained to think of politics as a career "*to go into*" via a Party which contains a sufficiency of friends and/or relations to adopt and foster the apprentice, and will eventually see him or her into the House of Commons on the understanding that the Member will adhere to his "*foster-Party*" through Office or through Opposition as may the Party's fortune or misfortune be.

Member's Sacred Conscience

This is an honourable profession, we are told, because the careerist has adopted (or been adopted by) the Party which holds the beliefs and principles nearest to our own (we can't hope to agree with *everything*, you understand). So, the beliefs "*nearest to our own*" concerning what is "*best for the people*" the candidate for election proposes to represent. The matter of the prospective MP's *conscience* which may prevent him from actually representing the voting majority who elected him was not mentioned whilst campaigning was in progress. Only when he is safely, if temporarily, installed in his Party seat does the paramountcy of *conscience* become obviously sacrosanct.

On the issue of capital punishment, for example: the voting public may periodically be allowed to express its preference for the return of this condign punishment for murder. But if it does it will wait until Domesday under the present system, for its wishes will always be thwarted by a sufficiency of liberal consciences among the docile ranks of Parties in all parts of the House. The Prime Minister's conscience will always preclude the use of a "*three-line whip*". That, they tell us, is politics, and they are right as the political ramp is set up today.

The question arises: "*What can I do about it?*" The answer is to understand the alternative and true meaning of politics, which is the art and science of building, or in our case preserving, a nation. Let us not waste our time campaigning, voting, backing, working or doing favours for any bespoke Party client soliciting our vote. Rather, let us do personally and privately whatever we can to preserve the integrity of our Race and Nation under God, and thus preserve our neighbourhood at least from the evils that threaten to overwhelm us if we do nothing.

It was once said that we had saved ourselves by our exertions and that we could save Europe by our example. Today we must set about saving ourselves from a more insidious enemy than a latter-day Napoleon Bonaparte.

We must learn how to counteract the perversion preached in our children's schools, in our Churches, in the media, in the Establishment. Teach our children what is right as opposed to wrong. Support like-minded neighbours in shops, buses, trains or wherever they express anti-Establishment opinions. Join with them in building and creating nationalist enclaves to promote right learning and living to circumvent the criminal damage being done to us by permissive legislation we seem powerless to change.

Read the next episode and find out how to save ourselves from the evils proliferating from the Abortion Act.

A

THE ABOMINATION OF LEGALISED ABORTION

THE screaming viragos who line the streets when a pro-life procession goes by would have us believe that procuring an abortion is a personal and private act. "Termination of a pregnancy," as it is euphemistically called, is "the right of any woman to do what she likes with her own body," the would-be murderess proclaims. This is patently not true. Despite all the efforts at distortion made by the whole gang of politicians and doctors who legislate and perform these acts (thereby making themselves accessories before and/or after the fact), it is impossible honestly not to recognise that the little body inside the womb is a baby; and since from the moment of conception nothing but food has been added to the fertilised egg, it always was a baby. **Deliberately to kill it is murder.**

Our society accepted the legalisation of this crime without significant protest, and the media (as we call our organs of mis-communication) have conspired to conceal the moral and physical ravages directly or indirectly caused by this now commonplace legal evil.

For the first time in their history, the English or those who act in their name have established laws to *allow* wrong to be done. Formerly the whole of their jurisprudence embodied the dictum: let *right* be done.

First was made a start in positively permitting wrong to be done and now there is no foreseeable end to it. Children are persuaded that fornication with contraception and/or abortion are "good for them." No one in the Establishment warns them of the physical and psychological damage that will result.

Women are exhorted to destroy any baby that fails to meet their arbitrary requirements in number, health, sex or mere social convenience. Now, the medical murderers want to justify themselves by "making life." Thus more fertilised seed is washed down the drain whilst "the creator" gets it right. How many lives did Louise Brown[2] cost?

The wanton destruction of our own race is ignored. We cannot go on being silent accessories to this genocide without losing our integrity. As long as it is permitted legally to murder the baby in the womb, what "right to life" has the baby out of the womb? If we continue to kill our own children, how can we claim the right to occupy our own land without let or hindrance from the floods of alien races legally and illegally *allowed* here (who for the most part, incidentally, do not practise legal infanticide).

The abomination of legalised abortion is the basis of all our perversions. It is the sin of Cain which if *un*repented will destroy our race as his was destroyed. In season and out of season we must proclaim this truth. However near and dear the would-be aborter is to us, we must not hesitate to condemn such an act as murder and prevent its commission if we can, whilst offering all other aid and sympathy.

Make sure that "family planners" and "abortion clinics" are exposed to the young as the murder promoters they are. Make "Save The Children" mean what it says. Save our own children instead of salving elastic consciences by "do gooding" in African states made charnel houses by colonial desertion.

If once we managed to force the legislators to deal with this crime as it deserves, we might find ourselves able to eradicate all other

---

[2] **Louise Joy Brown** (born 25 July 1978) is a British woman known for being the first human to have been born after conception by *in vitro* fertilisation, or IVF.

subversive permissions and enjoy a healthy Christian State again. Such an end is devoutly to be wished, but only persevering exertion can bring it about.

B

BANKERS AND BOLSHEVISM

ONE of the latest "vital issues" to be discussed and dissected with monotonous regularity is what is termed "education" in the Britain of today. Teenagers leaving the state schools, we are told, are too often and increasingly illiterate and/or innumerate. However that may be, one does not have to meet many ex-pupils of whatever age to become aware that even when they *can* read, write and reckon, they are still left to flounder through life without any initial instruction in the eternal verities or even in the hard facts of the usurious way of life we presently endure. Worse than that, for every one illiterate and innumerate product turned out by the national education system, there are probably a hundred or more *political* illiterates who will eventually comprise the voting population in any so-called Democracy.

An ignorant electorate is thus induced to vote for some almost equally ignorant person, selected to camouflage and perpetuate the oligarchy that finances itself by the age-old system of seemingly owning nothing and yet lending all things to all men - so long as they are prepared to pay the interest, of course! This is the "open" secret that is closed to all but initiates. This is the state of affairs in the affairs of state that is *not* known in schools, *not* studied in universities, and certainly *not* told in the press or shown on the ubiquitous "box".

Slay-Slide Towards One World

We few, who by the grace of God had enough right instruction or sufficient intellectual curiosity to discover the truth for ourselves, are denied even a public soapbox, let alone a housetop, from which to pass our knowledge on to others. The story of our slavery and the identity of our masters must continue to be declaimed from such private rooms and paper platforms as cannot be denied us, as long as it is necessary for the fiction of a "free world" to be mentioned.

1990 seems a particularly appropriate year to try once again to publicise how this wretched state of affairs came about in England, and to underline the role played by Bankers in the slay-slide we are on towards the One World that has been the goal of usurers ever since Eden. This is the little known and less celebrated seventh centenary of the expulsion of the Jews from Edward I's England. Seven hundred years ago, they were the bankers of their day. Living by lending money at interest was contrary to the laws obtaining in all Christendom. These first bankers were thus an "occasion of sin" which, it appears, weak Christians found it hard to resist even though the wages of their sin was often ruin. It seems hardly a coincidence that after the money-lenders' enforced and reluctant departure overseas, the value of the national currency (gold) issued free by the Crown did not alter for three hundred years. They were expelled from this land, bag and baggage, i.e. with all their money and goods, and forbidden ever to return because they had resented and refused every effort of the Church to convert them to the Christian faith which would, of course, have entailed the abandonment of their usurious monopoly.

Perhaps this ban on their immigration that has remained on the statute book to this day accounts for their return over the centuries since the so-called Reformation always in the guise of "Dutch" bankers or "German" bankers or indeed any other nationality that ensured residence in this country once usurious banking had been revived in legal form. We have only to consider our current homosexual and abortion laws to realise how popular legality can render acceptable a practice previously abhorred, which thus becomes destructive of the very fabric of the society that allows it.

Growth of the Money Power

The Elizabethan trickle of the money-lending returnees and newcomers became under Cromwell, a flood, despite his refusal to lift the formal ban on their immigration. Wars, especially civil wars, have to be financed; much better to have the financiers on the premises, so to speak, rather than having to travel bowl in hand to Lombardy or wherever the best interest rates could be obtained. The Stuart kings, the last of our true monarchs, were demolished and defeated by that same Money Power that Edward the Plantagenet thought he had banished forever. William of Orange was founder of the dynasty of puppets who have right royally confused their people to this day.

"Whenever failure looms, create a war" became the policy of all days. Six years after the Inglorious Revolution, the perfect instrument to nourish these was clamped on to a people who still speak of being "safe as the Bank of England" when they wish to exemplify the probity of any institution. The Bank of England was never anything but a Bank in England for founding and fostering a hydra called the National Debt. It began in an almost unnoticeable and unnoticed way: a few million pounds lent at five per cent interest to the Government of the country wanting to finance a war. No prizes for guessing who was to pay the interest of the hydra throwing out the heads demanded to defray the more pressing expenses of the War of the Spanish Succession, the War of the Austrian Succession, the American Revolution, The War of Jenkins' Ear, the Peninsular War, the Napoleonic Wars....

The Bolshevik Connection

"What has all that to do with Bolshevism?" you may ask. This: when a country of usurious residence becomes so debt impoverished as to be nothing but a ruin concealed behind a seemingly solid facade, it is time for the Money Power to move on to fresh woods before the inhabitants begin to identify the trees in the home park. In 1913, the

Money Power moved to the U.S.A., there to create with practised deviousness a fresh hydra called the Federal Reserve System. A National Debt by any other name is still a National Debt. Lo and behold! One year later the first world carnage began and in the midst of all the death and destruction seven more hydra heads sprang out of the neck in New York.

One of them was Bolshevism (life blood by courtesy of Kuhn, Loeb & Co. in the first instance). After that, it is difficult to move even a financial pebble without finding some usurious growth under it.

So what with Bolshevism and its respectable offspring, the Union of Soviet Socialist Republics, having done their stint with a Second World War, and a variety of multi-coloured revolutions having created a pile of wreckage where the Almighty Dollar used to be, it looks as if the Money Power is on the move again and might be going on a Yellow Passport instead of the rather tattered Red one. Are we to see Chinese chequers or a row of bonsai on the tables of the latest financial establishments?

C

CRIMINALS AND CONDIGN PUNISHMENT

"CURIOUSER and curiouser," said Alice, commenting on her odd experiences in Wonderland. "Stranger and stranger," we might say when we comment on the ways of the looking-glass land in which we presently find ourselves, where *everything* appears back to front.

Soldiers who in the course of their duty shoot some terrorist engaged in acknowledged warfare, are liable to find themselves standing trial for their own lives in the media, if not in court, with every likelihood of being convicted by manufactured opinion if nothing else, and every certainty of being covered with liberal odium. In "non-violent" contrast, the bombing-terrorist must not be shot out of hand and thus more often than not escapes apprehension at the time of the outrage and, if arrested later, is provided with all the apparatus of civil law to maintain his innocence "until proved guilty", regardless of the fact that he has proudly claimed affinity with and/or membership of an **Army** dedicated to war against the existing society. Thus, the soldier becomes a vindictive murderer whose terrorist victim is really a patriot who has possibly been too eager in his activities in pursuit of the justice denied him.

Thus is war waged today. Perhaps, however, if we had conducted the last world conflict on similar lines, we might now be enjoying envied prosperity under the direction of the leaders of our late "enemies" now residing in West Germany. After all, by our treasured liberal criteria the defendants at Nuremburg could hardly be said to have had a fair trial, could they?

The Limp Arm Of The Law

Well, what about civilian lawbreakers? We have even stranger ways of dealing with them. They, too, are regarded as "innocent until proved guilty". As persons bent on performing nefarious deeds seldom choose times and places when there will be onlookers and eavesdroppers assembled, there is almost invariably a certain amount of conjecture about the guilt of anyone suspected and detained. It is called circumstantial evidence and tends in liberal eyes to be even more suspect than the detainee. If the latter "confesses", the statement has been forged or the confession has been extorted by violence. If the accused claims the "right to silence", it must not be thought to show that he has anything relevant to hide.

If, despite all these safeguards, the detainee is charged, tried and convicted of a crime as serious as financial fraud, murder or complicity in a robbery conducted with violence, he will be sentenced to be housed and entertained in top security at the public's expense for an indeterminate period of years sometimes alluded to as a "life sentence", where he may enjoy amenities offered in the form of "connubial visits", radio and television, books, games and means to practise hobbies. Lesser criminals do not fare so well. They are overcrowded into insanitary gaols where they are liable to suffer violent and/or sexual assault and all the ills resultant on the corruption induced by smuggled drink and drugs. Even prisoners on remand are sent to these places to await trial because there is no room for them at the police station.

All this is an undoubted scandal which is a perennial cause of liberal concern, even attracting periodic attention in the media whenever seemingly unmanageable riots and revolts occur among the prison population, resulting in millions more pounds being added to the taxpayers' burden and much heart-searching (Enquiries) called for by what are somewhat ironically termed "the authorities". The "enquirers", we are currently told, have so far come up with "overcrowding" as being the main cause of the unrest, yet if there is a certainty in this world it is that no "authority" will be exercised in the direction of the alternative to imprisonment being suitable corporal and/or capital punishments - and even that mediaeval wickedness, the pillory.

Soccer Hooligans' Own-Gaol!

When I suggested to a friend this last measure - or the stocks - as a remedy for the wrecking of soccer games, he (who is the reverse of liberal) said it simply could not be done in our society as "there would have to be police protection from the missiles of irate neighbours". It would only provoke more riots. If this is indeed the case, then say I, put cages over the stocks/pillories as a concession to the lawlessness of the contemporary populace. Somehow, I do not see soccer hooligans persisting in disruption of the game if subjected to a sojourn in the stocks protected by cages but exposed to the ridicule of passers-by. And that would be a lot cheaper than rebuilding gaols to match five-star standards required by sensitive inmates.

A correspondent informed me last month that it is "religion we do not need". Maybe it is true that we do not need religion if that is some vague spiritual feeling, but we do definitely need religion if by it is meant belief and obedience to the triune God and the ultimate reign of Christ our Saviour, King of Kings. Only then will we understand that in this sinful world it is the duty of authorities, be they monarchs, presidents or dictators, to order their societies for the *general* good. Better for all for a villain to be despatched to the justice and mercy of God than for him to remain the unrepentant object of attempts at "reform" in an institution that of its nature appears to be designed to accomplish the reverse.

The "short, sharp" corrective might not have been needed if the original public school regime had been employed for all young people before they learned to "do their own thing" and if condign punishment, such as temporary confinement, birching, flogging and hanging, were invariably inflicted according to the offence. The taxpayers' money saved on "board and lodging" might then be profitably spent on providing hygienic "waiting" accommodation for remandees. Thus might society be made both happier and safer to the general good.

D

DEMOCRACY IS THE DEVIL - LET HIM HAVE IT!

SOME years ago, John Tyndall[3] was asked on television if he believed in Democracy. If the query had been phrased in Latin, it was evident that the questioner would have used the form which expects the answer "No". As the interview was conducted in what presently passes for English the interviewer had to rely on a sceptical tone of voice. Mr Tyndall, nothing disconcerted, replied that of course no government is possible without the overall consent of the great majority of the governed. In that sense he did believe in democracy. That commonsense reply resulted in the subject being abandoned for the rest of the interview which was, alas, only too predictable in these days when people's "freedom of speech" fluctuates dramatically in tune with the media notion of the "respectability" of the member of the demos in question.

Invention of Satan

Blasphemers, pornographers, murderers, thieves and vagabonds are all welcome to "air" their views in the names of liberty, equality and fraternity - those being the democratic ideals that fathered the bloody Terror[4] organised by Robespierre and St Just and its even bloodier offsprings reared by "the will of the people" from Manhattan to Moscow, from San Francisco to Saigon. But let one unenlightened

---

[3] **John Tyndall** (14 July 1934 – 19 July 2005) was a British politician who led the National Front in the 1970's, and founded the British National Party in 1982.

[4] "**The Terror**". The wholesale execution by guillotine of persons condemned by the arbitrary will of a revolutionary council called the *Committee of Public Safety* which horror brought an end to that phase of the revolution in France in 1789.

patriot among the demos raise his voice to condemn Democracy for the damnable (and damned) invention of Satan that it is, and the air vent is suddenly stopped. Communication is confined to the level of the strings and tins of our childhood attempts at telephony. The dominant sound bounced from satellite to satellite is the age-old howl induced by the Priests and Elders of the Temple: "Away with him," "Crucify him." The modern equivalent of that sentiment is: "Away with fascist beasts," echoed by multitudes every bit as treasonably managed and deluded as the one gathered before that vacillating time-server Pontius Pilate during the most famous mistrial in history (though the performance at Nuremburg ran it as close a carbon copy except that no Witness to the Truth was present on the later occasion).

That mob screaming for the blood of the Innocent only a few days before had been a joyful crowd acclaiming that same Innocent as their promised King and Saviour. How were they so easily persuaded to the opposite view? Why, "the Priests and Elders went among them" extolling the advantages of choosing a robber so successfully that against all legality, justice, compassion and integrity they chose Barabbas. Democracy had reduced the chosen people of God to an unthinking rabble who acknowledged no king but Caesar. Whence Caesar also was reduced to the dimensions of the feeble Governor of Judea ceremoniously washing his hands of the crime he had agreed with "the majority" to commit.

Democracy has done no less for us. The first democrat was Lucifer - not a "deprived" person lacking love and care but the very brightest creature in a harmonious hierarchy, only not quite bright enough to know that Heaven is unique. He fancied setting up his own establishment - Liberty. That made God redundant - Equality. So the masterless angel, having made Hell for himself and his followers, has busied himself ever since persuading mankind to join him in that state - Fraternity. He does not have to be an imaginative innovator in his sales talk. The same old lie serves to cripple the same Old Adam. All our so-called modern democratic methods are not variations on the original theme - they *are* the original theme, only the tempo is much slower since the Fabian enthusiasm for the inevitability of gradualness.

We should recognise the technique: it has been employed against our laws and institutions often enough. We do not have to go back two thousand years to recall it. The first key to the successful operation of Democracy is the abrogation of any restraining law - in our case, the Common Law of England, inspired by God and assented to by every subject under its protection. The next is the elimination by death or imprisonment of the personal embodiment of the law, be he judge or monarch. The last requirement is a brainwashed populace which will then accept its servile state as safe and normal. Our Common Law and our Constitution so rooted in it, are buried beneath such a range of nullifying expediencies as to be as invisible as a neglected grave. Though we still have a monarch, she is bound and gagged so tightly with synthetic conventions and human respect that she cannot even answer petitions from patriots wise enough to know they are desperate. We have no king but Ombudsman!

"They Went Amongst Us"

But surely not all our Priests and Rulers are corrupt. Oh no, we have a number of moderates. So did the Sanhedrin - one of them provided a sepulchre for truth. As to the brainwashed public: when confronted with the unmistakable treason of the European Community, even the be-spoke B.B.C. could not produce a favourable vote until we were all gathered in the Referendum forum where the High Priests and Elders "went amongst us" extolling the virtues of the robber - and against all loyalty, justice, integrity and even commonsense we too chose Barabbas. After twenty-two years brooding over Northern Ireland and four hundred years over usury, "they went amongst us" until we didn't know a traitor from a loyal subject; a debt from a credit; order from chaos. Oh yes, "they went amongst us."

No conference is complete without these flitting birds heralding the approach of the tiger ready to take the next bite of every nation's sovereignty. Cohn-Bendit[5], the prophet of "perpetual revolution" to Belfast; Burns of the "American" Federal Reserve to London and Basle; Kissinger to all stations from Peking to Pretoria; all fixing fresh shackles on the victims of "world democratic opinion". Every student of current affairs has marked their passage and yet, in the unlikely event of the Brain of Britain being asked what these plenipotentiaries have in common apart from globe-jetting at taxpayers' expense, he would hesitate to reply for fear of the Public Order Act!

There was a time when the British, and not only the British, were proud to call themselves subjects of the Crown because such subjection made them free under the Common Law. Even the eighteenth century rebellious Americans, though determined on founding a Republic, thought that law so admirable that they based their own Constitution on it. Now both written and unwritten Constitutions are in tatters. Patriots in both countries are concerned to piece them together again. Don Bell writes that when he left his native America in 1926 it was a Republic, but when he returned thirty-seven years later it had degenerated into a Democracy. Now it is said, democratically speaking, that the height of our ambition is to achieve citizenship of a godless world where we shall all be as Moderate-for-Truth as is compatible with human respect.

Patriots, however, have no such sorry outlook. We have seen that Democracy corrupts, and Parliamentary Democracy corrupts

---

[5] **Daniel Cohn-Bendit** is a French-German politician. He was a student leader during the unrest of May 1968 in France and has been a federalist (and controversial) Member of the European Parliament since 1994.

absolutely. Corruption is the best evidence that death is an accomplished fact. When we lose our fascination for re-arranging the ruins and bend our efforts to removing the rabble, we can uncover the ancient foundations and build our State anew with native stone. Let the Devil take Democracy - when we recover our own Monarch, our own money, our own law and our own land, we shall be happy to be British subjects of our once and future Sovereign.

E

E.C.U. J'ACCUSE

THERE is a novel by Georgette Heyer that vignettes what might otherwise be a totally forgotten piece of history. It is set in the nineteenth century and tells of a robbery of "the most perilous treasure ever known." The thieves, therefore, had to pre-arrange safe custody for it until it should be possible to spend it with impunity; for the ingenious tale turns on the peculiar nature of the newly minted coins that composed the target.

It appears that the government of that day, in a delicate and secret operation, was about to replace the abolished gold guinea with an innovation to be called the sovereign. Still a coin, still gold, but valued at twenty shillings instead of the guinea's twenty-one. The robbery is successfully accomplished during the first consignment's journey from Mint to Bank.

As the story was written in the early 1950s, it is probable that the author had based her plot on what she considered a unique historical quirk. However, a reader in the later 1970s might well have recognised in his contemporary government's metric con-trick an adaption of the age-old scenario reiterated in *The Tollgate*.

Whenever the lords of loan-creation find it expedient to de-stabilise an established means of exchange, they take care to disguise their purpose and to delay public recognition of the consequences for as long as they can. The success of their tactics depends upon the efficiency of the political and journalistic tools employed. So far, they seem to have gauged the necessity for subtlety to a nicety. When the anaesthetised public recovers its senses, the pain of the latest amputation is past and forgotten in some artificially induced euphoria.

The guinea was brought into existence at the instance of King Charles II with a value of twenty shillings, and never went anywhere but up until it reached thirty shillings in that significant year 1694, when the usurious Bank of England - pregnant with its monstrous offspring, the National Debt - came into being. By 1698, the guinea was back to twenty-one shillings, and was abolished in 1717. Like its inaugurator, it was "an unconscionable time a-dying," and so had to be killed off. Its successor proved equally difficult to dislodge; it took half-a-dozen Continental and one World War to do it. Thence things were easier.

Gold gave way to paper promissory notes to pay in more (and cheaper) paper. We were left with silver coinage - shrinking silver. Who can remember a five shilling piece being legal tender? Another world war, and silver gave way to cupro-nickel. With the disappearance of the silver threepenny bit and of the half-five shilling piece, the death of the English coinage and currency was only a matter of time. Like the guinea before them, have gone the sixpence, the wieldy penny, the halfpenny, the farthing, and lastly the shilling. One can only suppose that the imminence of the ECU[6] has made the redundancy of the two-shilling piece with its pseudonym "tenpence" unnecessary.

The only difference between the loss of our effective monarchy in the seventeenth century and the palpable surrender of our puppet monarchy in the twentieth century, is that the one was followed by the establishment of our alien rulers in a so-called national bank, whilst the other will be followed by the establishment of the same alien rulers in a veritable international bank in a land other than our own.

---

[6] **European Currency Unit**: the forerunner of the Euro.

The ECU is England's death certificate. It awaits only the doctor's signature and we shall be living in a mausoleum, for our country will be legally buried alive. Surely it is time to sack the doctor and try homeopathic medicine.

F

FAITH AND FREEDOM

THERE is what Helen Waddell calls "the innocent story" quoted in her book on *The Wandering Scholars* of mediaeval Europe: "Three clerks went on pilgrimage to sea without provision, that being God's business, only that the youngest said, 'I think I will take the little cat.'" She tells how they came to an island and halted there to recite the Psalms for the day and the little cat went down and fished for them a great salmon; how they doubted, not seeing the hand of the Lord in the paw of the little cat, until they roused again from their devotions to see the salmon brandering on the fire of coals, which brought them too near the shore of Lake Tiberias to doubt.

As a society we are too far from faith in God Himself to believe in His miracles. It is as if we left the feast thinking there was no more wine to be had there, and went and gorged ourselves on the raw "Spirit of the Modern Age" instead. Addiction to that spirit has done for the body politic what alcoholic rot-gut does to the drunkard.

Man's Hubristic Contempt

God does not do for us anything that, with His grace, we can very well do for ourselves. As someone has pointed out at Cana, Our Lord did not rub a lamp and summon a genie to appear. His mother said to the servants, "Do whatever He tells you," so they drew the water, filled the pots and carried them to the steward. How would the three clerks have fared if the youngest had not taken the little cat to do the fishing? But we are above all that! We think it is "childish things" we have put away but, as so often, our interpretation of a biblical phrase is at fault. We have put away the child's innocence and wonder, whilst clinging to the legacy of Adam's sin that festers like a cancer we obstinately refuse to have removed. So long as we refuse the baptism that will fill our souls with grace, so long shall we be denied the wisdom to avert threatened destruction by obeying the laws of God instead of legalising the lusts of Man.

The so-called "Greens" are the latest fashion in panacea production. We are commanded to press for political decisions resulting in Government action to ban the evils that have polluted Mother Earth and brought about the "hole in the ozone" causing "global warming." The "evils" to be banned at any cost are nuclear bombs and nuclear reactors, refrigerators, weedkillers, waste, sewage and scent sprayers. Above all, "ban babies" runs the recipe for global salvation. Only thus shall we make space and time to save the elephants, whales, tigers, barn owls and bats, together with everything else from wind flowers to wild orchids. In the resulting ideal One World, we shall have "saved" everything except "the little ones" and our own souls when the sum of all our sins again finds us out.

It is the global *warning* we should be heeding lest our abandoned race should again be reduced to a second Noah and seven companions - though this time we cannot be sure of even eight survivors since disgraceful Man has earned himself Babel and Babylon, Sodom and Gomorrah, and the destruction of both Jerusalem and the ancient Covenant between God and His chosen people. Over the centuries Man's sins have brought the wages of wars, plagues, pestilences, earthquakes and eruptions - everything except the once-and-for-all Deluge - and God's answer to that could be Drought!

Faith in Man has made us slaves; faith in God will make us free. If we still will not live free by faith in Jesus Christ, true God and true Man, and in the light of the Church He founded, we shall inevitably be enslaved in the One World envisaged by the perpetrators of the present chaos, which can only be the forerunner of Satan's hellish kingdom. If we will only return to the feast even when there appears to be no wine, we shall be there when the miracle happens. Nineveh repented; Nineveh was spared. Even Jonah was surprised!

G

THE GRADUALISM OF THE REVOLUTION

AS with Ian Smith[7], the verbal opposition of Mrs Thatcher to the prevailing "winds of change" in their respective countries has conferred heroic status in the annals of Right-wingism everywhere. They are both worshipped as political martyrs who did their best against impossible odds. Anyone holding a contrary view is dismissed as a prejudiced crank or, more gently, as one overdoing the conspiracy theory of history through misplaced zeal. The present writer figures in both categories, but remains of the same opinion still!

"It is all of a piece," as the cook said in some forgotten thriller. The mysterious Power that purports to establish universal hegemony in defiance of the Creator's Word and Will for fallen humanity's salvation and celestial destiny has pursued that aim by much the same method since our first parents' expulsion from Eden. Always the ultimate attainment has been periodically frustrated, not by contemporaneous society but by the wrath of God. So gradual and devious have been the recurring campaigns of successive pawns of the Devil in pursuit of his aspiration to world domination that nearly always "the little victims play," ignoring the evidence of approaching doom and disregarding any divinely inspired prophets sent to warn them.

---

[7] **Ian Douglas Smith**, (8 April 1919 – 20 November 2007) was a politician, farmer and fighter pilot who served as Prime Minister of Rhodesia from 1964 to 1979. He led the predominantly white government that unilaterally declared independence from the United Kingdom in 1965.

Emerging Pattern

In 1529 England was still a Catholic kingdom, despite Luther, Calvin or whoever else set up as the latest light of the world. Then the pattern began once more to emerge. The ambitions of a lustful, profligate king and a cold-hearted wanton opened Pandora's box.

In pursuit of his desires, Henry VIII forgot that he, like Pilate, would have no power if it "was not given him from above." With his abrogation of the power given to the Vicar of Christ on earth, he made the monarchy subservient, in the first instance, to the receivers of the wealth stolen from the Church, and subsequently to the bankers of those same receivers. He murdered, more or less legally, the only two far-sighted enough to visualise the end result of his abrogation: John Fisher, Bishop of Rochester, and Thomas More, erstwhile Chancellor of England. The unity of Christendom was shattered into myriad sects. Faith and charity were in eclipse and even hope died at last.

If all the bishops had seen what the dire result their "patriotic" obedience (if that is what it was) would have, would they have taken that first step on the long shuffle to the new paganism? Alas, they saw no harm in accepting their king as head of the Church in England. When in due time the Church in England became the Church of England, it was too late. The lay Catholics of England and the "hedge" priests died for their faith in their hundreds: the landed gentry were either martyred or fined into exile or apostasy. The "new rich" clung to their ill-gotten gains through restorations and regicide, evolving into the die-soft Tory "opposition" of today. Usurers returned and by the end of the seventeenth century had annexed the royal monopoly of the issue of credit. The Money Power ruled again. It took four hundred years to turn Christendom into the multi-religious and multi-racial stew that is Europe today. It took rather less time to destroy the intervening *imperial substitutes*, for the labourers in the colonial vineyards were quite as gullible as their predecessors.

If they survived the Money Power's tactical wars, they were too bemused 'with phantom victories to do anything other than bow before the "winds of change" despite all the latter day Fishers and Mores who told them to beware of the hurricane behind the zephyr.

The Message of Fatima

The last warning was given to three young shepherds in Portugal more than seventy years ago. With the miracle of the sun to help them, they did their best to persuade their fellow-countrymen to obey the exhortation to "pray for the conversion of Russia" and to believe the warning of the chaos that would follow a failure so to do. Though one of the shepherds is still living, the warning and the message have been shrouded in official silence. Far from praying for the conversion of anyone, let alone Russia, both pastors and people for the most part are busy acting on the palpably false assumption that Man is doing very well for himself, thank you. The unfortunate disorders today are merely temporary hiccups on the progression to universal justice and peace in the New World Order.

So now we are on the last lap. Are professing Christians really going to continue "doing their own (sectional) thing" until they find themselves so helplessly corrupt as to be fit for nothing but the slave quarters in this life and the fires of Hell in the next?

Surely not. There is still time. Remember: "the days will be cut short for the sake of the elect."

H

HISTORY - WHO CAN BELIEVE IT?

HAPPINESS, they say, has no history. To a large extent this appears to be true since all but the first three chapters of the first book out of over fifty volumes relating to the history of mankind, from his creation to the coming of God's promised Saviour, are concerned with the tale of disasters resulting from what befell our first parents in the Garden of Eden.

One dictionary definition of history is "the department of knowledge that records and analyses past events." Up to about A.D. 90 this is what the Testaments Old and New did because they were written by men who, however periodically delinquent, really were chosen and inspired by God Who made them. The records relate both the glory and the shame, rewards and punishments, victories and defeats of this people from Eden to Bethlehem, from Jordan to Rome.

The pagans also, who by the time of Christ's coming made up the majority of the world population, had strayed so far from the belief in the one true God they had no reason to deny or conceal their motive forces, which ranged from the search for Nirvana to the adoration of idols whose supposed appetites demanded regular human sacrifices. Still, always at the core remained some scent of the lost truth...a rumour of a woman with a child, somehow sacred, haunted the wings of the less bloodthirsty philosophies; and the idea of sacrifice to please or to propitiate. But nowhere in all those twisted faiths is it the *priest* who offers himself for sacrifice. The pagans also knew that it is the innocent victim who makes the perfect sacrifice. Paganism reached its apogee in the Roman republic and had passed it when its gods sank to being mere emperors.

Universal Hegemony

The vision of God's Chosen People also had shrunk from the pristine promise of eternal salvation followed by heavenly bliss to the mundane desire to be rid of hated Rome, and see in its stead themselves in universal hegemony. So when their Messiah did come, and was deemed unsuitable by all the "upper classes" except for Nicodemus and Joseph of Arimathea[8], it became essential either to bend, conceal or falsify the true story to any extent necessary to promote the desired end. This is what the perfidious Jews did then and have continued to do from that day to this.

When the "wise men came from the East" and asked King Herod of Judea where was he who had been born King of the Jews, the King sent for *his* wise men to ask them where Christ was to be born. He was told, "Bethlehem in Judea, for it was written by the prophet..." Immediately, deception began. When the wise men, being warned in a dream, did not come back "so that Herod could go and adore the child too," he killed all the boys in Bethlehem aged two years and under, and presumably never knew that Jesus with Mary and Joseph were long gone to safety in Egypt.

So for thirty years the Jews place-sought, plotted and quarrelled with the Roman Governor in comparative peace. Then came Jesus' public ministry; the teaching; the compassion; all those miracles; even people being raised from the dead! Everything showing that this was indeed the Messiah, the Truth, the Anointed One. Thousands of people followed him over the countryside; listened to Him condemning the moneylenders, the hypocrites, the self-righteous; running rings round the Pharisees whenever they tried to trap him into uttering sedition.

---

[8] **Joseph of Arimathea** assumed responsibility for the burial of Jesus after his crucifixion. He gave his own sepulchre to house the body of Christ. He was a member of the Sanhedrin.

We can imagine what would have happened if the Jews and not the Romans had been the ultimate authority. No appearing on the equivalent of television for Him - he made the interviewers look both silly and malevolent. After one highly successful rally (even with no Cable Street[9] mob to make it appear a riot) the High Priest and the Elders met in panic to find a way to put Him to death. To accomplish that end, they employed a traitor whom they despised; violated their own legal principles and, at last, in frenzy denied their own unique faith whose personification was standing before them: "We have no king but Caesar."

Timeless Technique

Look around today: the technique has not changed in two thousand years. When the soldiers deputed by the Chief Priests to guard Christ's tomb returned on the Sunday morning in a state of shock saying that there had been an earthquake and a dazzling angel had rolled away the stone from the empty tomb saying Jesus had risen, their employers could find nothing better to do than bribe them to say that the body had been stolen by His followers whilst they (presumably) were asleep! And that is the likely story the unbelieving Jews still tell today. It must have been one hell of a bribe! But seemingly, the Bishop of Durham accepts this feeble tale as history. Wonderful what reiteration through the available media will do, especially when enough time has elapsed to destroy the witnesses and produce a plethora of phoney evidence - or *vice versa*. Does that remind us of anything?

So what does history have to say about the Mystical Body of Christ? Yes - the Church. Well, up to the 13th century, what with the

---

[9] **Cable Street**. The scene of an attack by a Communist/Jewish mob on a ceremonial march of the British Union of Fascists, led by Sir Oswald Mosley, through the east end of London in 1936 which resulted in the passing of the Public Order Act 1936. This, among other things, included the banning of "political" uniforms.

profitable loan business provided by the financing of Crusades and other Christian enterprises, the Church had a reasonably good "press". However, the conscience of Edward I of England brought an end to all that. He is the "anti-Semite" responsible for the proto-Holocaust of the Expulsion. The Plantagenet's had not much luck after that; until the last of the royal line, Richard of Gloucester - after figuring in every English history book as a brilliant soldier from his youth; a loyal and beloved brother to Edward IV; the popular and just Governor of Northumberland - is then, without any evidence or explanation, depicted in those same history books as a hunchbacked monster who cold-bloodedly murdered his innocent nephews (his dead brother's sons left to his charge) to gain the throne which had been offered to him anyway. Minors as sovereigns posing likely levers for the ambitious were not popular in those more realistic times.

This *volte-face* becomes somewhat less inexplicable if the reader realises that the script was compiled by an ally of the usurping Henry Tudor; a remote family connection who by the aid of traitors triumphed in the battle in which Richard III was killed and the "crown plucked from a thorn bush." A subsequent glance into Henry VII's royal cupboard would have found it positively littered with skeletons of legitimate and pretended heirs to his usurped throne. Yet five hundred years later even the most ignorant student of what passes for English history "knows" that the last Plantagenet monarch was the most horrific royal villain ever, whilst Henry Tudor and his equally lethal progeny are "let off with a caution," so to speak, because they "broke the thrall of foreign domination (i.e. the Pope) and made England great."

All except Bloody Mary, of course. She burned heretics whom she could just as easily have had hanged, drawn and quartered for high treason, and by Bills of Attainder have recovered the wealth they had acquired via the stolen abbey lands. So it served her right, didn't it?

And Good Queen Bess disposed of Mary, Queen of Scots, rightful heir of England. She took a long time about it simply because she could not find anyone incautious enough to be an assassin for so dangerous a boss. So she had to put her own name on the death warrant of her legitimate cousin and sister Queen who had sought sanctuary with her from the Scottish rebels financed, not for the first time, by the powers behind the English throne. But... "Brutus was an honourable man." Elizabeth was a great English woman!

Having destroyed the authority of the monarch, the Money Power's next target was the monarchy itself. We possess it still but only in puppet form - and how long will that performance be allowed by "Europe"?

True Blue Ruin

The French have words for it - the more things change, the more they remain the same - and so it is with history. When liberals want to denigrate some ancient and worthy value, they exhort the rest of us to "keep up with the modern world" and admonish us for "trying to put the clock back." But we do not have to "put the clock back," as they say, to find the times quite as "out of joint" as ever Hamlet did.

It is all in Jane Lane's historical novel, *Gin and Bitters*. If you have never heard of Jane Lane[10], it will be because she has revealed so much unpalatable truth in the scenery surrounding her fictional characters that she has been automatically consigned to Establishment oblivion. *Gin and Bitters* tells of the ever-rising, ever-disappointed hopes of the British people for honourable government. It covers the period between the "Glorious Revolution" of 1688 and the Georgian

---

[10] **Jane Lane** (1905–1978) was the pen name of **Elaine Kidner Dakers**, a British historical novelist and biographer. She is best known for her books about the Stuart period and 18th-century Scotland, written from a Catholic and Royalist perspective. A prolific authoress, she wrote over 30 novels and biographies.

aftermath of the burst South Sea Bubble. The parallels with our own experiences between another revolution (or possibly the same one) of 1917 and the terrorist horrors of our own day are indeed terrifying - but also edifying in showing how induced "mass thinking" usually ends in the massacre of the "thinkers," if so they can be called with any degree of accuracy.

The central figure of Jane Lane's story is a secret and pamphleteering Jacobite who spends his life in post-Stuart London, clerking for one who today would be termed "a good Conservative" - a kindly brewer who provides his clerk with a pittance and an attic where he can spend his leisure writing the truth of the revolutionary outrages daily committed against unwitting people "resolved to live peaceably under William III." He did not write to incite any violence, but to convince the people that the restoration of their true king "is necessary to their interest, to show them what they have lost in losing their lawful sovereign, to warn them of the practical evils they must expect under the kind of government which now rules over us, and to set forth as well as I am able the advantages they enjoyed under the ancient monarchy."

He pursues his vocation through the reigns of four figure-heads; through the dissipating of the legacy of ale-drinking "Merrie England" to the war-torn, debt-ridden, gin-slinging realm of George I. Through the evils of the prototype of unnecessary wars, credit monopoly, unpayable debt and financial chicanery, he lives his lonely life and pens his true commentaries. From first to last, his is a labour of love with no reward in this life and the gallows to end it. And yet, in so far as he influences anyone, it is to that one's betterment. Therein lies the antidote to despair.

But to the parallel. Just as the gullible mass of peaceable Britons in the twentieth century suffer the treachery of Major and Kinnock, alien invasion and usurpation of power - *any* outrage of sovereignty, in fact, rather than be dubbed "right-wing extremists" - perennially hoping for better times after each change of government figureheads, just so seventeenth century Englishmen suffered the treachery of John Churchill, the deposition of their true king and the usurpation of "Dutch William". They did this all in the propaganda-induced belief that the first and the last would save them from the terrible tyranny of James II's "ravening popery" - a plague more to be feared than bubonic. They did not like William of Orange, but consoled themselves with the "safeguard" provided by his marriage to Mary Stuart, their deserted king's daughter. This tenuous link with legality served to comfort them with the illusion of continued monarchy, while they meekly acquiesced in the edicts of the secret oligarchy that survives to this day. They were unlikely to demand "their king again" so long as they thought they had one. Do we hear the echo of Mr "Common Market" Heath proclaiming that Britain merely exchanges her sovereignty at home for the same sovereignty in Europe?

Those "Dutch" Bankers

Twenty years before, England had been fighting the Dutch. Now the Revolution forced her to accept a Hollander king and to take a principal part in his personal vendetta with the current "wicked man" of Europe - Louis XIV of France. To this end, the French "subsidies" were exchanged for the "benevolence" of so-called "Dutch" bankers, who in 1694 enabled the war-impoverished English to finance the Grand Alliance (c.f. United Nations?) in its belligerent operations in Europe. The Bank of England was established by its loan of five million pounds to the unsuspecting public. There was no discrimination - it was open to everybody to pay the interest. It was a national debt, or rather *the* National Debt.

So the fruits of the Glorious Revolution of 1688 were soon institutionalised: a foreign war to eat up the national income, a foreign debt to feed the foreign war, a "national" bank to swallow all local banks and nourish the foreign debt to feed the foreign war; and to wash down all the woe with the least comprehension on the part of the victims - gin. Gin, the outlet for Holland's surplus barley; gin, the imported "blue ruin" that bankrupted English brewers and befuddled English wits; gin, sold over the counter in drinking dens and under the counter in grocers' shops to the debauchery of the young and the poison of the old. Today it is heroin that comes over the narrow sea.

The sole beneficiaries of this lamentable harvest seem to have been the issuers of the credits and surpluses, so it is worth recalling who were the financiers of *this* revolution that was alleged to be the triumph of the Protestant Reformation. Says the "with-it" brewer's son, "I have a profound admiration for the Jews, since they are the fathers of commerce and did indeed invent the banking system. Moreover, without them we never would have had the Revolution, for Suasso[11], of whom you may have heard, lent King William two million pounds for his expedition, and Sir Solomon Medina, his banker, did likewise." Clearly the forerunners of Kuhn, Loeb & Co., without whom we might not have had the Bolshevik Revolution!

The son continued: "A bank begins to confer some real advantage to the realm only when it lends out the money it receives from this man to this other man who has need of it and will make it productive, and *by creating money by means of banknotes and figures in a ledger* [our italics] a bank quickens the nation's trade and keeps the circulation of cash flowing freely." Now *that* is a Tory sentiment if ever there was one, but the conservative brewer is not impressed. He thinks he can invest his money unaided and imagines that all such usurious practices are temporary and will come to an end when their "own Stuart Princess Anne is Queen." The Whigs see to it that he is disappointed. The war continues almost throughout her reign, each

---

[11] **Francisco Lopes Suasso, second Baron d'Avernas le Gras** (*ca.* 1657 – 22 April 1710) was a banker and financier of the Dutch Republic. He was also known within the Sephardic community as **Abraham Israel Suasso.**

victory more expensive than the last, culminating in a dukedom and a palace for the traitor John Churchill and a Debt now swollen to fifty millions in twenty years. And still the people will not demand their lawful king.

The Turn of the Tories

A recuperation period is required; at the tail end of Anne's life it is the turn of the Tories. We are now on very familiar ground. Harley and St John, having insinuated themselves up the backstairs to political eminence, set about making an artificial silk purse out of the Whig sow's ear. Allegedly Jacobites, they brought down the Duke of Marlborough, without whom there could be no war, and arranged a peace with France, both sides guaranteeing the Protestant Succession - even Jacobite Tories did not want a king who awkwardly remained faithful to his religious conviction when expediency demanded compromise. Harley and St John's "perks" were the Earldoms of Oxford and Bolingbroke. Here the Tories fell out "on a matter of principle". Bolingbroke ousted Harley (shades of a 1940 Churchill and Neville Chamberlain), but was unlucky enough to be outmanoeuvred by the Whigs gathering round Queen Anne's death-bed and found himself isolated with only his Jacobite horse, who obstinately refused to drink the water of apostasy. Bolingbroke was impeached on the very treaty that brought such long power to the Whigs and was approved by them on two subsequent occasions.

With the accession of "German George", who reigned in Hanover and spoke no English, the Revolution was consolidated, the Whigs were triumphant and the Party System was born. The people were again thwarted of their rightful king because the Tories, no less than the Whigs, had settled for a puppet monarch who would obey their will.

A piece of political and financial chicanery called the South Sea Company adopted by Robert Walpole, First Lord of the Treasury, brought untold wealth and political supremacy to him, scandal to his bribed ministers and ruin to the uninitiated when the great South Sea Bubble was burst. Robert Walpole bought and sold so secretly and betrayed his fellow-conspirators so ruthlessly that he, who had both blown up and pricked the fraudulent Bubble, was the only character to emerge from the ensuing maelstrom with a fortune to rival the Incas' and an enhanced reputation for prudence and integrity amidst his countrymen's orgy of greedy gambling! Two hundred years later, the same would be done by and said of one Bernard Baruch, afterwards called "the uncrowned king of the United States" and the acknowledged adviser to five presidents. *His* bubble is known in the history books as the Wall Street Crash.

A Hollow Conservatism

Nowadays, no country considers itself free without a Bank to create "credit"; a Debt to create "working capital"; a Stock Exchange to "work" the working capital; and the whole economic anthill to - what was the phrase? - "confer real advantage on the realm." Two more wars financed by the "admirable Jews" have added accruing benefits. Now we have an *Inter*national Bank and *Inter*national Debt to make the universal wheel turn to everyone's advantage.

So why are the denizens of these fortunate realms so dissatisfied that whenever they are enduring the benefits of Whig, Socialist, Democratic or Conservative Revolution, be it bloody or bloodless, they have to have the possibility of a return to Conservatism dangled before them to prevent a *counter*-Revolution of devastating consequence? There have been Whigs and Tories; Liberals and Tories; Socialists and Tories; Communists and Tories. Significantly, it is the "true blues" who go on forever. The ruin may acquire a little more ivy, but it remains essentially a ruin.

The Thinking Few

The really hopeful thought about all this is that the people as such are never going to change anything. They are always going to be innately uninterested in politics - that is how they have fallen for the party racket. Although they will always hanker after a king endowed with "the authority that comes from above" and bemoan the outrages committed against them in Democracy's name, they are never going to do more than dream of salvation when next a Conservative opposition brings a return to some mythical good old day.

It is hopeful because it means that the votes of the masses are not only not necessary, but positively detrimental to the promotion of good government. Even a few persons of integrity endowed with true authority and the courage to wield it can restore the ruins of their nation's integrity. It is only necessary for them to *lead*, i.e. to go first, when they get the chance, and not to herd and drove.

It would be very odd if the gospel analogy of people with sheep were not eternally apt. It has lost its efficacy only because we have been taught to think of a good shepherd as one standing afar off, whistling the sheepdogs to round up the flock into an enclosed space. In those circumstances the sheep, always manoeuvring to escape canine vigilance, never look where they are escaping to, and victory goes to the one with the most experienced dogs. It seems we need to emulate the Best Shepherd; even if the leader ends on the Cross, the followers do at least see where to go and will follow a man rather than be herded by a dog.

I

ISCARIOTISM AND OUR UNSCEPTRED ISLE

IT can hardly be a coincidence that the only traitor among the twelve apostles of Our Lord Jesus Christ was the "intellectual" whom they considered eminently suitable to "manage the funds" of their small society. He was their banker - although his house was not that of Maxwell[12]! It was not, however, the love of money that was at the root of his evil. Rather it was the same vice as Satan's - the pride that made him think he knew better than God how to manage, not just the funds, but the whole of human society. And when he found he was wrong, he still did not acknowledge the omnipotence of his betrayed Master. If he had, he would have known that repentance would make his sin forgivable. But as he could not forgive himself he remained, in his own mind, "better than God" who would have been "soft" enough to have forgiven him as He forgave Peter.

As for western society, it has long ago decided it knows better than God. Even though the resultant humanism has produced nothing but chaos in Church, State, education, industry, urban and rural economy, and all its scions and dupes have yet to admit that what they are doing is the ultimate evil that, unrepented, will be deserving of the suicidal climax such persistence in self-idolatry will surely engender.

---

[12] **Ian Robert Maxwell** (born **Ján Ludvík Hyman Binyamin Hoch**; 10 June 1923 – 5 November 1991) was a British media proprietor and Member of Parliament . Born in Czechoslovakia, he rose from poverty to build an extensive publishing empire. After his death, huge discrepancies in his companies finances were revealed, including his fraudulent misappropriation of the Mirror Group pension fund.

Christians For Zion

That is western society. Then what about Zionist society? Is that not on the right track - back to fundamentals and the right way home? Recently, the post brought a packet of information and pleading on behalf of a society called "Christian Action for Israel", asking for a "Wall of Prayer for Israel" to be built around the world. This society, according to its 1991 newsletter, was founded by one Basil Douglas Jacobs, a "South African" it seems, whose life "became a refuge and example to many who were seeking to follow the Lord God of Israel". This statement was followed by the remark: "In addition, Basil's faithfulness to the local church of Jesus Christ earned him the respect of church leaders."

The rest of this somewhat specious document purports to be a history of the land of Israel, full of quotations from the Old Testament about the Second Coming of the Messiah "to restore the Kingdom of Israel". Such statements, it says, "only confirm that modern Israel is a biblical phenomenon". Well, if you can believe that... Somewhat further on we read, "Only when Messiah reigns over the world from Jerusalem in fulfilment of the Davidic Covenant will her borders finally and forever reach that of biblical proportions."

So that is what we all have to pray for: not for the conversion of the Jews but that this righteous people "that has never been an aggressor" will rule the world from Jerusalem! The only thing wrong with all this is that there is no mention of the breaking of the Davidic Covenant because of the repudiation and crucifixion of the Messiah in His First Coming. It seems that Zionist society like western society (with which it is not unconnected) has the same inhibition in refusing to recognise the signature of the One True God in the Blood of Christ. It is, in fact, adamant that it has done no evil of any kind. On the contrary, Zionists claim to be, as they say, "the victim of Christian animosity and anti-Semitic persecution". It is the perpetrators of the resulting "holocausts" who will never be forgiven but remain objects of vengeance and a source of "compensation" until bankrupt of life or property. Thirty pieces of silver, after all, would hardly buy a potter's field today, let alone the world - well, not without compound interest!

The Old Testament tells us that in Eden Adam and Eve "walked with God". After Abraham's covenant the Israelites were ruled by God represented by Judges. Time came when God's Chosen People tired of having only a Judge and asked for a King. Another step away from God's direct rule, until finally they arrived at the Sanhedrin and its majority rule which voted death to their rejected Messiah. Kingdoms tend to be the norm in Christendom too, but we know what has happened to both. Christendom is abandoned to Babel and kingdoms to democracy, and all seemingly bent on destroying themselves in despair. Again, it was not a coincidence that in the early '60s United Nations Day ousted the Feast of Christ the King from the last Sunday in October.

For us Humanism has had its day. Poor creatures, we have reached the edge of the abyss. We can be destroyed by our own vice or we can call our King again and have all things added. What we are doing is not unforgivable if only we recognise our own errors and repudiate them. God's mercy is always available but we have to ask for it with humility and a firm purpose of amendment. There is no other way to escape the fate of Judas Iscariot.

J

JUSTICE AND PEACE?

NO one nowadays has to be a "believer", as they say, or a committed church-goer to become aware that in the very realm that used to be God's own domain, the conception of God in His Three Persons - Father, Son and Holy Ghost reigning supreme over heaven and earth and in the hearts of those that love Him - has given place to that of Man. Man, the self-made apogee of the process of evolution which continuing over uncounted millennia has transformed him/herself from a lump of almost inert jelly, a prisoner in the primeval slime, into the complicated masterpiece of natural, scientific enterprise we see today. Man is "walking tall", ruler of the earth and ready, in the politicians' phrase, to establish the New World Order which will, in the church-man's phrase, result in an equally new era of justice and peace.

Autocracy of Man-Made God

This optimistic forecast accompanying the proclamation, emanating from who knows exactly whom of a decade of evangelism, has been greeted and repeated with fervent appeals for action by spokesmen and ministers, priests and preachers of variegated religious sects all round the world, and not least by the supreme head of what until quite recently was universally known as the Catholic Church, adamantly claiming to be the one true church founded by Jesus Christ, the Word of God made flesh, who came, in the words of Wisdom 18 (14-15) quoted in the Introit of the Mass said on the Sunday within the octave of Christmas: "While all things were in quiet silence and the night in the midst of her course, Thy Almighty Word, O Lord, leaped down from heaven from Thy royal throne."

So how has it happened that the Church founded by God-made-Man has become a front runner in the cause of the autocracy of Man-made-God? Any readers familiar with the tale of the age-long machinations of the Money Power in politics will have little difficulty in recognising on the religious platform the same plot, type-casting and direction as those which hypnotised the captive audience applauding the performances that presaged on the world stage destruction of all it held dear.

Consider the example of Great Britain and the British Empire as they appeared in the last act. The whole body politic was riddled with usurers eating away like worms in a rotting corpse, but to the courageous men and women who lived, worked, fought, taught and made those alien lands their home, the "body" still looked almost as good as new. It is said that only in war or under the threat of war will people consent to give up their freedom, but it appears that more than the threat or even war itself is necessary to persuade people to relinquish their own freedom to benefit some alien characters whom they have no particular reason to love - rather the opposite. So the victims must be made to put themselves in the trap.

The manoeuvres performed to this end between the years 1919 and 1939 resembled nothing so much as the con-trick called Find The Lady, usually to be seen performed in the sleezier parts of fair grounds. Friends and foes, allies and enemies changed sides and positions with such bewildering rapidity that one never knew from one day to the next what thimble The Lady was under. The world audience emerged in the dark, having seen two monsters called Stalin and Hitler put under the spotlights while two more waited in the wings. Two knights in shining armour had star parts: Franklin D. Roosevelt across the Atlantic, proclaiming the inviolability of American neutrality whilst in conspiracy with Winston Churchill "in the wilderness" in England, goading "the under-study" Neville Chamberlain to bring down the curtain on the first scene with the declaration that would change the theme from peace to war. And so he did. And we all gave up our freedom. Victors and vanquished alike were in seemingly irredeemable hock to the usurers whose "interest" demands are seldom confined to mere money which they can make for themselves anyway.

Church Follows Empires In Its Fate

Now we are all captivated by an adapted version of the same play - or should it be ploy? The potentates in shining armour and the kings with hollow crowns have been re-cast as prelates with triple hollow crowns above their "civvy" clad ministers. It took a long time with many hiccoughs on the way, but at last the One True Church is in as parlous condition today as the European empires were fifty years ago. We could still save it, but not if we fail to recognise the face of our enemy behind the masks of Pacelli/Churchill, Spellman/Roosevelt, Montini/Macmillan, Wojtyla/Thatcher, etc. Sort them out for yourselves! Even the "safety valve" is cloned by Cardinal Ratzinger.

When a play is as successful as this first one described above, it becomes a classic to be revived and adapted to fit the contemporary circumstances. But... "Those who have ears to hear, let them listen."

"Who made you?" "God made me." "Why did God make you?" "He made me to know love and serve Him in this world and to be happy with Him in the next."

That way alone leads to justice and peace so conspicuously lacking in the domains bemused by the ideals of liberation theology and rendered chaotic by the seeking first the Republic of Man. It is enough to make the Devil laugh.

If the parallels in the foregoing sound fantastic, and even if they do not, the proofs and details of this maze of betrayal are available in a remarkable book[13] whose author, Mary Ball Martinez, was Vatican correspondent for *The Wanderer, National Review* and *American Spectator* for fifteen years. Her revelations are as shocking as were A.K. Chesterton's in his *New Unhappy Lords* when that first appeared.

---

[13] The Undermining of the Catholic Church (1991).

K

KINGS AND KNAVES

IN what used to be known as Christendom, kings are people who not only reign but rule their subjects according to the immemorial laws of God, the Creator of all things, visible and invisible. Knaves, in this context, are the people who, behind a royal facade, enslave both kings and subjects under the law of usury. According to this criterion, the last king of England was James II, son of the murdered Charles I; and the last "king" in any country was Salazar[14] of Portugal. After them has come first the trickle, soon the torrent and now the deluge of unrepayable debt that has flooded the whole world and deprived of real estate everyone except the usurers.

The seemingly universal blindness of the slaves to their bondage under the, at present, inescapable dominion of debt has been accomplished through the usurping Power's use of a series of euphemisms that have deceived perhaps even "the elect", certainly the duped populace. In the Money Power's parlance: A bank is a place in which one puts one's valuables and cash for safe keeping. Credit is what is advanced by banks to set up commercial enterprises until their profits accrue to replace the capital expenditure entailed. A loan is a temporary accommodation enabling the borrower to anticipate the advent of some expected endowment by either sale or inheritance of goods or property. Money that the "workers" earn or the "drones" inherit is issued by the Government to facilitate the exchange of

---

[14] **António de Oliveira Salazar**, (28 April 1889 – 27 July 1970) served as the Prime Minister of Portugal from 1932 to 1968. He also served as acting President of the Republic for most of 1951. He founded and led the Estado Novo (New State), the conservative anti-liberal government that presided over and controlled Portugal from 1932 to 1974.

goods and services. The greatest euphemism of them all is that Britain is a free country ruled by an anointed sovereign.

The fallacy of this last supposition was once more revealed to those with eyes and ears to see and hear one morning this month when BBC2 had exclusive coverage of the State Opening of Parliament, which contained the newly elected Commons, the majority Party in which had formed the Government from amongst its members. The session was opened by Her Majesty Queen Elizabeth II of Great Britain and Ireland etc. There, presented in "glorious technicolour", was all the panoply of power; the ushers, the heralds, the consort supporting the crowned monarch in all her robes of state. She proceeded slowly and solemnly towards the throne on the dais in the House of Lords from which she would deliver the speech outlining the programme of legislation proposed by the ruling Party for enactment during the life of the Parliament just assembled.

We are ruled, we are told, by the Queen-in-Parliament - but not, it appears, in the House of Commons. No monarch of England has been allowed in that House since, in the 17th century, King Charles I was turned out from it with contumely by his own subjects, soon to make war on him and later to murder him by Commons' law. So to open "her" Parliament, which she has not called and may not dissolve on her own initiative, Her Majesty must go to the House of Lords to read a career politician's speech to the House of Commons, whose majority selected him from the 649 other career politicians to hold the office of First Lord of the Treasury, i.e. Prime Minister, for five years or until such time as himself decides to "go to the Country" for re-election or is himself rejected by the members' vote.

The anomalies do not stop there. The Treasury holds no treasure but merely administers the amounts of scrip originating in the hallowed precincts of the Bank of England that have been "created" and issued at interest to transitory governments, who consequently cannot govern but can only obey the behests of the pipers who pay them to call the appropriate tune. And there, we come to the knaves. The source of their will goes all the way back to Eden and the expertise to further it undoubtedly derives from the same ruthless Satanic intelligence that beguiled our first parents out of Paradise. Still, to borrow from Shakespeare, the Devil would still be talking to no purpose if "nobody marked him". But his minions presently dominate every front. No need to consider any country but England or any reign but the current one.

A Reign Of Shame

When Elizabeth II was called back from holidaying in Kenya in 1952 on the death of her father George VI, England was a Christian country with appropriate laws for keeping her so. Her colonial empire and her daughter dominions overseas still operated the system of Imperial Preference which gave complementary trade in a market of over 600 million. Her scientists and engineers, adventurers and pioneers were among the foremost in the world, conquering mountain heights and ocean depths; farming and fishing were still healthy, and ships, aircraft and automobiles were produced competitively.

Forty years on, Christian order has been reduced to pagan chaos. The Queen swore on oath at her coronation to rule according to the laws and customs of her people, but she seems to have ruled according to the dictates of the only real power in this world: the Money Power. It offers the carrot in the form of comfort and "correctness" and if that is refused, as in the case of Edward VIII, the stick in the form of bad press and banishment. The Queen has given her assent in writing to all the Acts of Parliament that have turned our "right little tight little island" into a multi-racial, multi-faith, vice-ridden sorry state. Today's pro-Euro-rhetoric will do nothing but hasten our submergence in an immoral morass in which children are taught "safe sex" rather than the three Rs; the results of female fornication are financed by reluctant tax payers supporting "one-parent families"; the Hippocratic Oath no longer applies to the treatment of babies in the womb; sodomites are now a protected species; "consenting adults in private" have become pederists parading in public; and "doctoring" the human genes is about to become big business.

What has become of the young Princess who broadcast from the Union of South Africa (not yet a pariah) on her 21st birthday dedication of herself to the service of her people? The knaves have been at work. Her consort and her eldest son, the heir to the throne, are both products of Kurt Hahn's Gordonstoun where they trained to become assiduous One-Worlders, attending secret directive meetings of the sinister Bilderbergers; nor should we forget the Mountbatten influence. The Duke of Edinburgh was seemingly always available to attend ceremonies to haul down the Union flag in abandoned colonies while cracking jokes with "leaders to darkness and death" like Jomo Kenyatta. Friends of the family were Armand Hammer and Averill Harriman, capitalist-communist supporters of the first order. The Duke and the Prince are co-directors of the World College, inaugurated to teach the next generation to accept global satanic reign with equanimity, if not enthusiasm. This long campaign reached its zenith with the approval speech delivered to the European Parliament by Her Majesty on the subject of the United Kingdom's orderly progress, via Maastricht, towards obliteration in the confines of United Europe.

If anyone doubts the satanic influence behind all these betrayals, we can only remember that the Devil's disciples cannot help boasting of their power and allegiance. In the 'fifties it was "the Devil in the Queen's hair" that was engraved in her portrait on Canadian dollar bills. It was removed only as a result of a campaign of protest started by *Candour's* founder, A.K. Chesterton. We are reminded, too, of the cabbalistic sign made on the wall of the cellar at Ekaterinberg when the Czar of Russia and his family were ritually done to death there by order of the Bolsheviks.

We must accept this salutary reminder. Democracy has been achieved with singularly little opposition, so if there is to be a last stand, it is only from the demos it can come. We cannot expect to be saved by a citadel that has already fallen. We have been in the last ditch a long time now. There is no point in deserting the firing step as long as we have even a single weapon to wield, for after all we know the Devil cannot win. He was shot down on Calvary nearly two thousand years ago and has never really stood a chance since.

L

LANGUAGE AND LIES

AT Babel, the "being as good as God" enterprise looked as if it were about to succeed, and the Devil's disciples at last seemed capable of proving the truth of Satan's prophecy concerning the effect of swallowing the fruit of the Tree of Knowledge so hopefully tasted in long lost Eden. Nevertheless, since that first disobedience Man had seemed incapable of sustained "knowing good", being so often pre-occupied with, not only knowing, but practising *evil*, until God lost patience with him and his wickedness and put an end to each and every persistent and recurring attempt at usurping His divine authority. So on this occasion, the Tower builders on the eve of success suddenly found themselves "foreigners" one to another and all co-operation became impossible. They no longer spoke the same language.

Through the centuries, all subsequent efforts at overriding or undermining the Creator's rule have sooner or later been frustrated by Him in equally unexpected ways, always making it "back to square one" for the plotters.

Deprived Of The Truth

Today, we have once more arrived at the brink of the establishment of yet another New World Order, and although it is being presented against a backdrop of almost universal chaos, there is no protest from the heads of the apparently powerful states and organisations who would not ordinarily be expected to abdicate in the face of such fragmentation. The answer to the conundrum is that the master-builders employ the language of lies and understand one another perfectly; it is the people who do not understand anything because they have been deprived of the truth through double-dealing in what was founded by Our Saviour Himself to be the depository of Truth.

7th December 1941 is perhaps recalled as the darkest day in the history of the United States, when they were manoeuvred by their own President into unwanted, unnecessary war by a concealment of the Japanese intention to attack Pearl Harbour. The top secret Japanese Navy code had been intercepted since late 1939 and the decryptions armed Roosevelt with the knowledge that would have enabled the U.S. to beat off any Japanese attack. His deliberate withholding of information proved even more effective than any lie in preventing the mass of American people from knowing what had been done to them and by whom. Chicanery was never officially admitted, as witnessed by the unremitting efforts of the American and British authorities to suppress the archival records that would throw light on the disputed aspects of the Pearl Harbour scandal. The political scene was thus set for the half-century of Satanic conspiracy culminating in the collapse of civil order amid a raging religious disorder.

Twenty four years after Pearl Harbour, the Fathers of the Roman Catholic Church were tricked into conniving at a similar devastation on the field of the Second Vatican Council. Chicanery was never officially admitted, and until now never even unofficially admitted. The shocking revelation comes in the April 1992 issue of the Abbe George de Nantes' *Catholic Counter-Reformation newsletter*, in which he states that on 7th December 1965, "Satan entered the Church never to leave again until the day of Christ's coming in glory through the intercession of the Immaculate Heart of Mary."

Here is a summary of how it was done. There was in the Council called by John XXIII a great conservative mass which, if the Modernist heresies were to be implanted in Catholic doctrine, had to be strangled practically at birth. The first manoeuvre to this end occurred over the theme of reform of the sacred liturgy, allegedly to make it more acceptable to the people of our times! Nothing is sacred to Modernists. "The poor peasants had not understood the Mass for centuries" was the theme. The long and complicated debates which should have been subject to the rule of secrecy were "leaked" to the media in familiar political style, and so were converted into worldly "democratic negotiations" which resulted in compromises effectively disguising the needed capitulation of the conservative majority. The manipulators, by not following the time-honoured Council Regulations when only theological opinions were the issue, made the flouting of them so customary that it passed unnoticed when outright heresy was to be insidiously introduced in the latest equivocal texts.

Deceived By Perfidy

On that fateful day, 7th December 1965, when the Constitutions promoting Religious Liberty, Man's Equality with God, and his Fraternity with Satan were to be adopted into the Church of Christ by Paul VI, they were received with seemingly unanimous approval by Fathers enchanted by the rhetoric and deceived by the perfidy of the Vicar of Christ, to them as much "above suspicion" as Judas had been at the Last Supper. The Faith-destroying declarations were actually signed, in ignorance of manipulation, during the Pope's eulogy on the supremacy of Man, delivered instead of a homily, in the middle of the Sacrifice of the Mass. By the time it was ended, Satan was *in*[15].

How many lessons do we need before we learn to recognise the cloven hoof beneath the robes of state? However, it is not just princes who are not to be trusted: we should surely have some suspicion of prelates and potentates. When we experience the results of their official tenure we might at least guess what beastly extremities might

---

[15] For more details of this tale of deception, please see *The Catholic Counter-Reformation in the XX Century*, nos 246 and 247.

be hidden under their skirts or hats. Perhaps only a return to adoration of the one true God will give us sufficient acumen to save us from believing the lying language of such really unconvincing idols.

M

MONARCHY OR THE MONEY POWER

HOW right was Anthony Benn when he announced in the middle of the Maastricht futility that "if the Monarchy ever does go, it will be European federalism that does it, more than democrats like myself." Under the Maastricht Treaty, he said [*Sunday Telegraph*, 13/12/1992], "the Queen becomes a citizen and has a vote in the Euro elections. How you can swear an oath of allegiance to another citizen of the European Union has never been fully explained."

Presumably, it was not thought necessary to explain it, since for centuries now the British people have not had a monarch at all. They have been conditioned to accept a crowned puppet who performs at the pull of invisible strings manipulated by the arcane force known as the Money Power. Today, it appears, even that charade is becoming daily more redundant. When the alleged monarch agrees to pay income tax, she has obviously opted to proclaim herself "an ordinary British citizen", ripe to join her fellows in the amorphous flock being shepherded into the European pen, where even the trappings of sovereignty must, of necessity, soon be relegated to some suitable museum.

Authority To Rule

If a monarch is not an absolute monarch, then he or she is no monarch at all. In these islands up to 1688 and except for the Roman occupation, we have had *kings* and *queens*, were they British, Saxon, Danish, Irish, Scottish, Norman or English. Even the occasional usurper had the blood royal in his veins, even if it was a trifle thin in the case of Henry VII. They all ruled in the traditional way: issuing currency for the promotion of trade and the provision of national enterprise. Christians and pagans alike recognise that the rulers of any society - kings, chieftains or whatever their titles - appear to be imbued with the requisite authority.

The Christian anointed kings, indeed, knew that their authority derived from God and that they should rule according to Divine Law. It has been called the Divine Right, and was much misinterpreted by parliamentarians clamorous for democracy. However, it is not only Christian rule that derives from the will of God the Creator: "You would have no authority...if it were not given you from above," said Jesus Christ to Pontius Pilate. So: *all* individual authority comes from God, but nowhere does it appear that parliaments or "the people" enjoy the same patrimony.

From the fall of Rome to the Inglorious Revolution of 1688, apart from the Cromwellian interlude, monarchs who were deemed unsatisfactory for one reason or another were sometimes compelled by the Baronage, backed by the Church, to comply with a written agreement, such as King John and the Great Charter. Other times they were forced to abdicate in the face of insurrection by an ambitious relative, were imprisoned and subsequently murdered as was the case with Richard II and his usurping cousin, Henry Bolingbroke of Lancaster, afterwards Henry IV.

Thereafter, *his* grandson, Henry VI, was deposed, reinstated and finally defeated by Edward of York, also a grandson of John of Gaunt, in the Wars of the Roses. Lastly, Richard III, Edward's youngest brother, was killed in battle by another usurper and remote relation, Henry Tudor, who as Henry VII married Edward IV's daughter Elizabeth and founded the Tudor line. Thus far, the only rebellious attempt to saddle and bridle a king with a parliament had been Simon de Montfort's against Henry III, and that was frustrated by Henry's redoubtable son Edward, afterwards the First, who rescued his country from money-lenders by expelling them bag and baggage, thus safeguarding the national currency for another three hundred years.

The Tudor Disaster

It was the greedy Tudors who undermined both Throne and Altar. Henry VIII usurped the Divine Authority, debased the currency, stole the Abbey lands, bred diseased children and confused the Succession, thus laying his country open to the ravages of robbery and usury that, in turn, lead to debt, democracy and the death of monarchy. This last, like Charles II, was "an unconscionable time a-dying", but eighty-seven years from the death of Elizabeth I the Catholic faith in England had been virtually fined and executed out of existence; the Abbey lands were stolen and (irony of ironies) soon flooded out of the royal robber's hands into those of the venal lords who were soon in hock themselves and found betrayal more profitable than loyalty.

When the last true heir to the English throne - Mary, Queen of Scots - had been executed by the last barren Tudor, the only material for monarchy left was the son of the Scots Queen, nurtured from his cradle by his mother's bigoted enemies who had betrayed her to eighteen years imprisonment, ending in death on the block. With the reign of James, the Sixth of Scotland and the First of England, the ancient monarchy was on its last but one gasp. James' vices and "the favourites" engendered by them did nothing to recommend the monarchy as a Divine Right, and his popular son Henry died when a young man and left only "Baby Charles" with his stutter and his French Catholic wife, Henrietta Maria. He had so many disadvantages and never the means to overcome them. He had to defend his wife, his friends, his religion and his throne. His wife he saved at the cost of his friends, his throne and his life. His religion and his realm were given over to every extreme of puritanism. The monarchy has been proscribed to this day.

By the aid of the Commons, their King was tried, condemned and executed illegally with all the legal trappings. An army - Cromwell's - killed him. Another army - General Monk's - "restored" his son, Charles II, and yet another army destroyed Charles' brother, James II - that of his son-in-law William of Orange (invader), and his friend John Churchill (traitor). The last true King of England died in exile. The monarchy had ceased to exist, except as a dynasty of puppets who right royally confused their people. Instead, the Money Power ruled, as it does today, except that Queen Elizabeth II is the first Royal to proclaim her resignation in its favour.

N

NEVER IN THE NEWS - UNTIL IT IS HISTORY

THE adult innocents at home and abroad who largely make up the so-called Western nations appear to be nearly, if not wholly, convinced that accurate and detailed information is conveyed through the media on every subject - even politics - though it may be thought necessary, perhaps, to read several newspapers and listen and look at a selection of the newscasts and comment that abounds on radio and television to obtain a "balanced" view of the current happenings that will, they imagine, mature into history.

Nothing, it seems, will change the generally held opinion that at least one or more of the broadsheets will report without bias upon the day-to-day doings, triumphal or disastrous, of the famous or infamous that occur in all spheres thought to be of interest to the public at large. And yet, and yet... "Mud sticks" and "out of sight, out of mind" are two aphorisms that might give us pause when we consider who and what are celebrated *ad nauseam* or, alternatively, sunk without trace, and how much deserving of either extreme are the subjects selected for the treatment.

The Ubiquitous, Iniquitous U.N.

One has only to listen to a David Irving lecture to realise that what is passed down to posterity as history via the media, as often as not, bears little or no relation to the facts of the history it is intended to distort. The myth of the Holocaust is now probably too famously infamous to need any more refutation, but lately the public has been daily bludgeoned with "news" of the absolute necessity for intervention by the United Nations in the internal affairs of various countries in Europe, Asia and Africa supposed to be incapable of managing for themselves; none is too little known or too far away for international attention.

It is iterated and reiterated that only action on the part of the "peace-makers" of the U.N. can curtail the dreadful consequences occasioned by the crack-up of communist and/or colonial control. The U.N. must "save" refugees, presumably by removing them to become problems elsewhere; the U.N. must make "peace plans" and bring about "cease fires" in the various war zones by the use of some extremely irregular troops having nothing in common but the blue beret, and all apparently directed by the likes of the mysteriously surviving Owens and Carringtons, whose recurring failures are blandly explained away as necessary stumbling blocks on the road to universal peace.

Latest it appears that the interloping forces being subjected to lethal attacks by "the natives" have been given licence to defend the "peace" by engaging in retaliatory war! Some "natives", of course, are less intimidating than others. The shambolic U.S. led peace forces, though possibly capable of dealing with Somali clans, have not yet dared to intervene in Europe, since Europeans have always been the toughest opponents, which is why they have so often been tricked into fighting one another instead of combining against the universal enemy whose chosen aim is to mongrelise the world.

What a shambles is presently in prospect, but why should anyone be surprised? Some of us have seen this scenario before, but it has only recently become "history" and thus to rate media mention.

On February 26th there appeared in the *Daily Mail* under the banner headline, ONLY GOD CAN SAVE OUR NATION NOW, an expose of the past and present condition of the erstwhile Belgian Congo, the dolorous nature of whose "freedom" caused the *Mail* correspondent, Ann Leslie, to say: "What even ten years ago was unsayable: 'independence' has been a disaster for Africa."

Murder, Mayhem and Mansions

Only now do we read that Zaire, once the Belgian Congo, has "the biggest thief in history" as president for life[16], put into power by a C.I.A. backed coup in 1965; so that twenty-eight years later even the media tycoons cannot prevent some truth welling out. The Congo has been disintegrating for all that time. Road and rail networks return to the jungle; telephones and turbines are almost moribund; schools and hospitals collapse because, said some engineer, "the word 'maintenance' exists only in two African languages - English and Afrikaans." Although this robber president makes European insider traders look like public benefactors, the West continued to pour aid into his coffers despite the outrageous scandals of the Mobutu murder and mayhem accompanying his wholesale confiscation of his country's wealth translated into chateaux, mansions, castles and cash in Switzerland, France, Belgium, Spain and Portugal.

Even this tale of Black barbarism cannot be reported without a swipe at the Christian monarch and his people who built a country worth pillaging.

"A century ago," claims Ms Leslie, "the image which haunted the nightmares of the people living on the crocodile-infested banks of the Congo River was that of Queen Victoria's cousin, the rapacious King Leopold of the Belgians, whose agents smoked the heads of

---

[16] **Joseph-Desiré Mobutu**; 14 October 1930 – 7 September 1997) was the military dictator and President of the Democratic Republic of the Congo (which Mobutu renamed Zaire in 1971) from 1965 to 1997. He also served as Chairman of the Organisation of African Unity in 1967–1968 and became notorious for corruption, nepotism, and the embezzlement of between US$4 billion and $15 billion during his reign, as well as extravagances such as Concorde-flown shopping trips to Paris. Mobutu presided over the country for over three decades, a period of widespread human rights violations. He has been described as the "archetypal African dictator".

recalcitrant slaves and stuck them on picket fences." Wot? Not in gas chambers? "Today," says the gullible Ms Leslie, "King Leopold has a worthy successor in the man who now rules the former Belgian Congo."

So what did happen in the Congo in the 1960s when it was "in the news"? The Belgians were subjected to the now familiar liberal campaign for the liberalisation of oppressed peoples, animals, birds, fish, butterflies, bats and bears. No matter that they had established and governed a happy, prosperous, peaceful state out of the immemorial darkness that was Africa before the White man came. They were tricked or bribed away from their responsibility and the immediate result was insurrection, mutiny in the army, rebellion and rapine following so closely upon one another as to give the unmistakable impression of long term planning effected other than in the jungle.

Murder, pillage and the inevitable raping of White women, plus the last rebuff: the refusal of the British Government to allow military assistance to be sent from Northern Rhodesia when it was requested by Tshombe, the Katangan leader, to help him protect *his* people and the White refugees from the chaos of neighbouring Congo. That brought the final panic scramble of the remaining Europeans to refuge in neighbouring states, whilst the triumphant mutineers ran amok and the rest of Black Africa rejoiced at the Whites' abject humiliation.

Enter the United Nations. Lumumba's Black republic was recognised and instantly made a member of the U.N. Immediately there was an allegedly spontaneous mutiny of the "Force Republique", whereupon the Force's Belgian C-in-C and all his Belgian officers were removed from duty and the "mutineers" set to work to terrorise the Belgian community and drive all Europeans out of the Congo. When the Belgian Government at last sent the Belgian troops into the territory again to restore order, Lumumba screamed that they were "making war on the Congolese people" and called for the United Nations troops to come to his assistance.

Force Macabre

A.K. Chesterton's comment at the time was: "The composition of the first contingent of troops to be sent into the Congo represents for the Western European nations a kick in the teeth without precedent - an insult of such gigantic proportions that it is difficult to find words strong enough to describe it. The force was made up of soldiers from Ghana, Guinea, Mali, Sudan, Senegal and Tunisia. I do not know much about the Tunisians although one can guess what their outlook would be, but for the rest, the United Nations is sending savages to control savages. The Senegalese in the First World War did well at the Front, but their record of murder in the base areas of France was also formidable. Every European in the Congo will have been well advised to clear out before their protectors arrive."

To the macabre tunes called by the U.N.-U.S.-U.S.S.R. manifestation of the Money Power, the European civilisers abdicated one after another at the behest of their own governments, until today we are left with an "aid" and AIDS-ridden world, so obviously a disaster area that even what A.K. Chesterton called "our unpardonable press" has to say *something* other than "more of the same" - and what it has to say is unprecedented:

"There are no excuses left for Africa, no scapegoats from the past to blame any more. As the Ghanaian writer Ayi Kwei despairingly points out: "The sons of the nation are now in charge after all....When will the West come and save us? But the West has 'cured' itself of colonialism - and by curing itself of this 'evil' it has, in effect, condemned a continent to a living death..."

Or is this bluff statement only permitted because the task of colonial *and* home demolition is reckoned to be completed and no man's land ready for occupation and control by the New World Order? Well may we all say: Only God can save our nation now. But He will not do it for cravens.

O

OVER THE MOON

IN bygone days it was the habit of Heads of State, when they found themselves in any domestic difficulty, to provoke either a declaration of war or an "intolerable" insult from some unpopular Royal neighbour, so that in the excitement of retaliatory hostilities, the local unrest would be forgotten. In these days, owing to the prevalence of so-called democratic governments, it is usually necessary for the overall directing Power to find some other more plausible and transient distraction.

The spectacular advances in all branches of technology, financed by entrepreneurs in all theatres of war, make it possible for both the alleged victors and the undoubted vanquished to be destroyed or promoted according to the demands of the next phase in global manipulation.

For decades after the alleged end of World War II the manipulators found it necessary to take the people's minds off the anomaly of the concurrent Cold War and the Space Race. When East is East and West is West and never the twain should meet in peace, it was, of course, imperative to conceal from the gullible public the fact that both had been founded and funded by the same mysterious munificent power - the Money Power.

"Oh dear, the Russians have beaten us. Yuri Gargarin is the man of the new age," was the rueful greeting of American Space-Agers. But not to worry - we had manager Kennedy who had promised a revitalised team; the Moon in no more than ten years. There was euphoria all round - and they made it. Moon walks, space stations, recoverable shuttles, no limits, next stop Mars. The Russians were not such bad fellows after all. With co-operation, we could all go together: dogs, monkeys, women, ethnic minorities - all must populate the realms of Outer Space.

Poor little Earth was left rudderless as an abandoned ship until suddenly even the rats had nowhere to go. The latest "lift-off" fell out of the sky into the deadly, mourning hush, and "the people" were in the news once more. "The Brits" revived. The Imperial corpse arose and defended its second last pocket of Empire. The Americans were concerned with the economic Yellow Peril.

So the Cold War began to melt. The Russians had been so kind and considerate over NASA's debacle that it would not now be necessary for Americans to beggar themselves with Star Wars, went the media comments of the 'eighties. Rather should they concentrate on unity and co-operation, as the Europeans were doing with Common Market trading hopefully to peace and prosperity; resuscitated economies reviving in racial, religious and cultural harmony.

Whilst everybody had been Moon-gazing, the world had been manoeuvred quite a distance along the backways to the Money Power's goal of One-[Devil-dominated]-world. The post-World War II European Coal and Steel Community had progressed through Benelux, EFTA, the Common Market, the European Community to Maastricht and the European Union.

Now that the world seems to be teetering on the brinks of national triumph or of international disaster, we are back to square one. At the back end of 1993, the Americans' eyes were once more focussed on Space, Moon and Mars, whilst Britons, having been divested of all finance for modern defence, exploration and invention, had their eyes directed to "the war in our own back-yard", i.e. the demonstrably phoney "peace discussions" in "the Other Island".

The Americans, in the meanwhile, have gone through UNO, NATO, GATT, and most recently NAFTA to rapprochement with crypto-Communist Russia and the new WTO [World Trade Organisation], from whose decisions US manufacturers will have no appeal. What a familiar ring that has!

This loathsome progression has been achieved without significant protest from disintegrated nations and with active but clandestine co-operation of the puppets masquerading as "the freely elected representatives of the people". It is time - more than time - for the threatened people to stop looking in media-managed directions and to concentrate on their own salvation. Do let us get over the Moon syndrome and organise our own defence.

Once we comrades are ever aware of the Enemy's strategy and tactics he will be defeated, since it is plain that our blindness is essential for the Devil to prevail. Let us get going, see and conquer!

P

PANDERING IN PORNOCRACY

AS so often before, consultation with the *Shorter Oxford Dictionary* produces some "odd ball" definitions of words commonly used in one sense only. We tend to think of panders as people who procure, and or "run" prostitutes to satisfy the sexual appetites or aberrations of their customers. However, it appears that panders can minister to "the baser passions or the evil designs of others". "Prostitution:- to sell for base gain or hire". "Justice was prostituted in the ordinary courts to the royal will":- 'Greene; is the example given, and a pornocracy is entered as the name given to the Government of Rome in the first half of the tenth century.

It now rather unmistakably appears that pornocracy is the name that should be given to the Governments of both Great Britain and the United States of America in the twentieth century - and before - but the latest century will do for the enlightenment of the mis-indoctrinated young men and women of today. The children, alas, will continue to be subjected to such real-teaching until they are released from "heretical" education. "Heretical being that which is at variance with that which is orthodox in philosophy, religion, politics, science or art'.

The administrators of the evil designs of others have been in situ, masquerading as the representatives of "the people" whenever rulers, be they hereditary, elected or selected, put themselves in the hands of the usurers. Usury, it cannot be too often repeated is the crime of lending currency at interest for the financing of unproductive enterprises. There can be no more unproductive enterprise than war unless the levying of interest is the lender's business.

As some of us know, this situation was obtained during various periods of history ever since, and probably before, the worship of the Golden Calf was inaugurated by the Chosen People as soon as Moses took his eye off them when God called him to a conference on Mount Sinai. The results of such subjection have always been disastrous for the mortgagees but all too often they have hugged their I.O.U's and remained helplessly blind to the cause of their slavery.

The British people have reacted no differently from any others, except for those among the "forlorn hopes" of nationalists scattered round the bank beleaguered world. They alone have defended themselves and the faith with "head, heart and gun" no matter what the cost. Of these obstinate crusaders one could say that Leon Degrelle[17] was the noblest nationalist of them all without fear of discovering feet of clay in his boots - and yet, if he is known at all to succeeding generations, it is probably as a dastardly villain "wanted" for heinous "war crimes" invented by the Anti-Nazi League or the hounds unleashed by Comrade Wiesenthal.

The twentieth century has witnessed successive destructive campaigns by the reigning usurers conducted to complete the reduction to impotency of those nations as yet still operating on the aftermath of their once wholly Christian civilisation. Their economic impotency will unless repudiated, make them incapable of resisting the final obliteration of even their own national consciousness.

So soon as the twentieth century opened: the death of Queen Victoria saw the accession of the profligate, debt-ridden Prince of Wales who as Edward VII was signatory to the *Entente Cordiale* with France, and thus laid the explosive train that resulted in the destruction of two

---

[17] **Léon Joseph Marie Ignace Degrelle** (June 15, 1906 – April 1, 1994) was a Walloon Belgian politician, who founded Rexism and became a foreign volunteer of the Waffen-SS (becoming the leader of the 28th SS Volunteer Grenadier Division Wallonien). After World War II, he was a prominent figure in promoting National Socialism and Historical Revisionism.

generations of the youth of France, Germany and Britain in the carnage of 1914-1918 and 1939-1945. The simultaneous and progressive elimination of monarchy in all but name was attempted and accomplished. First by the extreme measure of the murder of the Czar of all the Russias and his family by money-powered terrorists. Secondly. by the elimination of the Royal ability to rule their now bankrupt countries. Failing either of these two ploys: contrived abdication of the more obdurate, such as Leopold of the Belgians and Edward the Eighth of Great Britain was found feasible. After that, there is always control by "Constitution" as exampled by Queen Elizabeth II. (Prime Minister Callaghan announced in the House of Commons that it is "the Commons" that rules the country. He meant of course the House of Commons not the common people; but even that is a lie.) If Her Majesty had shown any signs of rebellion, there was always the fate of His Royal Highness the Duke of Windsor to point the awful warning - or was the Ekaterinberg slaughter still the most effective rein?

The next tactic in this relentless war of attrition - the real "cold"war - was the circumvention of every nation's attempt to escape, such as: Imperial Preference and the free trading alliances (barter) of Germany, Italy and Japan. Imperialists, nazis, fascists, nationalists all were branded as criminals guilty of every extreme from racism (anti-immigration), persecuting of consenting adults (re sodomites and abortionists); indoctrination of the innocents (i.e. teaching the one true christian faith and practice).

Lastly the political defences of the so-called West were dismantled by careerists, terrified of earning the soubriquet "anti-semitic" by denying the monstrously propagated story of the Holocausts. Six million, ten million, X million Jews were daily proclaimed victims of endless torturing hatred by anyone or nation daring to defy the might of the usurping money power.

Simultaneously, the Red monster engendered by the illicit union of dollars and democracy, named the Union of Soviet Socialist Republics was reared, financed and equipped with all the weapons designed by the unholy lights of perverted science to ensure the slavery of the now faithless millions in West and East alike, and still the media power of the "evil designers" prevents the full horror of these betrayals from impinging effectively on the consciousness of the doomed nations.

There are still dedicated political soldiers in the field. The antidote to despair is to join them and determine to emulate as far as we can our national heroes past and present. We can still save our country by our exertions and others by our example but only by putting on the armour of the faith, calling upon our warriors Archangel Michael and St. George our patron, whilst imploring the aid of Our Lady Help of Christians, that she will crush the Devil's insolent head and enable us to obtain the peace that is in accordance with the will of God. There can be no salvation without war on wickedness.

Q

QUEER QUACKERY

IN an article in *The Daily Telegraph* of 26th June 1994 Myles Harris, described as "a London G.P." discussed the pros and cons of counselling under the title *The Quack Fix*. He began by stating; "Medicine has always tried to keep faith with the scientific model: observation, measurement, theory and testing. If the facts upset the theory then the theory must be thrown overboard. *"Death rates have plunged"*. He says, "Today nobody expects his wife to die in childbirth, or to see tiny coffins on the way to the cemetery. Two hundred years ago both events were commonplace". Babies, once born, it seems are presumably now 100% safe from infant mortality. But what death rates have plunged? Dr. Harris goes on to discuss "counselling and an explosion in alternative medicine therapies". Never a mention of the change from "tiny coffins" to the lorry loads of aborted foetuses, without benefit of coffins, carried across cities, countries and even continents to fill the factories and 'scientific' research establishments with the wherewithal to supply cosmetic firms with "improved" beauty preparations; scientists with expendable experimental material: eggs for implant in any "infertile" or lesbian womb whose owner applies for one or more.

Certainly they did not figure in childbirth. They are the results of the murder of healthy but as yet unborn babies. These crimes are euphemistically called "termination's of pregnancy". Then there is the murder of deformed or diseased babies out of the womb; this is called euthanasia. An item in the same newspaper on 5th July reads:

BABY'S KILLING TESTS DUTCH LAW

"The killing of a severely deformed new-born baby by lethal injection is set to become a Dutch test case on infant euthanasia. Prosecutors have begun the final stages of an inquiry into the death in March 1993 of Baby Maatje, who was born with hydrocephalus, an exposed spinal cord and leg deformation in Purmorend, near Amsterdam. A.P."

Even more bizarre is the case of the "lesbian lovers" whose "partners" were artificially inseminated because "they did not wish to go through the (to them) distasteful process of having sexual intercourse with a man; and yet another lesbian lover of a lesbian "mother" was granted "full parental rights" after the "father of the child", who had agreed to inseminate the lesbian once a month until she "fell" pregnant, now finds that the Child Support Agency does not recognise his "legally and unenforceable abrogation of his parental duties" will try to recover maintenance from him!

This is Baby Choice, a precious 4 1/2 month old little girl, burned by the saline solution used to abort her. There are 4,000 babies aborted each day in America, (one every 20 seconds). Abortion is legal thru the ninth month of pregnancy.

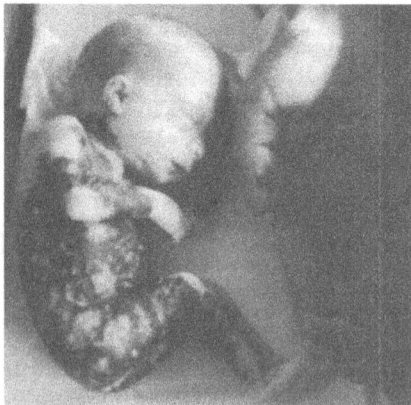

We have been led to believe that having an abortion is removing a mass of tissue. LOOK AT THIS LITTLE GIRL[18]. She is a perfectly formed human being! IS THIS SUCH A GOOD CHOICE?

How many doctors one wonders now take the Hippocratic Oath, which was promulgated some two and a half thousand years ago, part of which reads:

"The regimen I adopt shall be for the benefit of my patients according to my ability and judgement, and not for their hurt or for any wrong. I will give no deadly drug, though it be asked of me, nor will I counsel such, and especially, I will not aid a woman to procure abortion..."

Can it be that, unlike Sodom and Gomorrah, we have not yet been destroyed by fire and brimstone because our "cities of the plain", have not reached the apogee of wickedness of those by the Dead Sea? Perhaps it was not only the sea that was dead, perhaps those Sodomites had also added the gruesome destruction of their own offspring before they ever saw the light of day *and* had then advanced to the ultimate crime of malforming God's creatures to match man's self-distorted image?

God has never yet repeated himself so what fate awaits the unrepenting destroyers is quite unimaginable.

This terrible trail of perversion once followed "darkly at dead of night" became a "noonday devil" on the morrow of the establishment's unprecedented legislation to allow the performance of acts of buggery by "consenting adults in private".

Back to the *"Telegraph"* of 26th June 1994, which reported:

---

[18] Photograph and text with acknowledgments to Victory for the Unborn, P.O. Box 690762, Houston, TX 77269-0762. U.S.A.

GAYS BRING COLOUR TO THE CAUSE

"...an unfamiliar multi-coloured rainbow (*sic*) flag is flying from poles and balconies in many parts of London." "...the newly adopted banner of Britain's homosexuals...". "In Soho's Old Compton Street, London's gay centre, businesses are already using the (flag's) design on cards and advertising leaflets".

"There has been a steady demand since we started bringing them in 14 months ago but in recent weeks they have really taken off".

"David Baker, a gay journalist who flies the flag from the window of his Islington flat, said local residents had reacted very positively".

And just to reassure everyone:

"Inspector Robert Beckley of the Metropolitan Police's Community Affairs Branch, said he hoped the flag's popularity would not lead to attacks by "a tiny minority of yobs and bigots who seek to make life difficult for our gay and lesbian community".

"Luckily we live in a relatively liberal society" he said, "as more and more people fly the flag they should find support in numbers."

If ever a city asked for fire and brimstone or whatever else is likely to strike from Heaven, our capital has.

R

REVOLUTION IS RIGHT

WE are apt to speak of "The Revolution" meaning the French Revolution of 1789 or the Russian Revolution of 1917: then there are the countless revolutions that occur with almost monotonous irregularity within individual new "states", civilised or uncivilised, in any part of the world. To a vast number of people revolution is the overturning of an established system of government, regardless of the length or brevity of its foundation, but if one understands that Adam's was the first catastrophic rebellion that lost to him and all his descendants the earthly paradise, leaving mankind to roll from iniquity to iniquity seemingly as helpless as canoeists without paddles, hurtling down the rapids until they reached the comparative calm of the seemingly endless order achieved by the Romans over most of what was "the known world" of that day. The one and only Christian Revolution came into that world with its innumerable "household gods" and - to be on the safe side - one shrine to the "unknown god". It was *the* Revolution that was also the Revelation long promised to God's chosen people, waiting then in the Roman province of Judea for the expected Messiah, but a people with an *un*expected canker in its vitals.

REDEMPTION

In silence, at dead of night, "Thy almighty word, O Lord, leaped down from heaven from Thy royal throne". Christ Jesus, Son of the living God, born of the Virgin Mary, truly God and truly man came into the world to turn it from its pagan path on to the way of Truth and Life: to fulfil the Covenant made with His Chosen People to redeem them from the fatal consequences of Adam and Eve's original sin; to offer them His Way, Truth and Life everlasting. It need not have been the way of the Cross, unlike the Angels, the Chosen were given a second chance, but when it came to the choice, as a people they did no better than their first parents. They wanted freedom from Rome rather than freedom from the thrall of original sin; The kingdom of this world instead of the next. "He came unto His own but His own received Him not. But as many received Him, He gave power to become children of God". (Gospel of St. John). The choice is still open to everyone. One has only to study the calendar of saints to find that out. Anyone who asks will be received, from the "good thief' (Dismas) onwards. The rebellions against the New Testament will be no more successful than the rebellions against the Old Testament. After the "infiltra(i)tors" induced the Chosen People present before Pilate to proclaim that they had no king but Caesar, it was given to the Gentiles to spread the Word they had received from the faithful few under the leadership of Peter and the successors of Peter.

The Rock remains. Even a Vatican Council crammed with subversives and their dupes will never hear the Vicar of Christ pronounce *ex-cathedra* as infallible truth, a modernist lie, however firmly he may hold to it in his private capacity. "The Gates of Hell shall not prevail", so there can never be another revolution. Man's salvation has been accomplished - on the cross - since we would have it that way - and the Devil has been in the toils ever since, but *he* never gives up the struggle, so it is up to the true revolutionaries - us - to exhibit the same constancy with ever greater grace-given energy, since we know that only desertion in the face of the enemy can bring about our defeat. And that would be the deserter's own personal defeat: the Revolution will go on until the end of time.

THE REVOLUTION WILL TRIUMPH

One Worlders, then are never going to win. So, the Revolution will triumph whether we are here long enough to see it or not. Presumably, the view from the next world is much rosier. Anyway, since the Revolution is right and we are certain of victory, the war is a just one, and demands our participation.

The first necessity of the prosecutors of conflict is troops. Since it appears that we are engaged in a long war, perhaps life-long war, we must not be daunted if enlistment is slow; we can improve the situation if we think of the children as potential recruits and train them in the family to know that, as "the penny catechism" put it, we are here to "know, love and serve God in this world and be happy with Him forever in the next". We shall, in all probability, soon have young enthusiasts who will think that the first duty of those who would "serve God" will be to fight His enemies - those being the Devil and his agents whether they are in this world or from the nether regions of the next. That being the case our recruits will be, as were Baden-Powell's original scouts, only too anxious to "be prepared".

The "preparation" demands schoolmasters, ready to proclaim the truth of history in the face of "Establishments" determined to subvert it with every violence necessary. One thinks of the long-line of latter-day martyrs in this cause: Ezra Pound, Bob Mathews, Joe McCarthy, Whittaker Chambers, Huey Long, Fr. Coughlin, Ernst Zundel, Malcolm Ross to name only a few. They risked their livelihoods - and sometimes paid with their lives or their liberty. They form a calendar of secular saints and are inspiration for us and for the generations to come.

Nor must those now in the front-line (pun-intended) relax. We must be ready to storm financial redoubts; set up insulated enclaves; hold fast to whatever we own; help others to repossess their heritage. We are not in the business of defending *their* back yards but in war to regain our motherlands.

It cannot be a coincidence that St. George is most often depicted slaying the dragon and St. Michael slaying the serpent so perhaps our final exhortation should be in the nature of the "speech before Agincourt" only rather more comprehensive as it emanates from the Church Militant:

"Holy Michael, Archangel, defend us in the day of battle. Be our safeguard against the wickedness and snares of the devil. May God rebuke him, we humbly pray, and do thou, Prince of the heavenly hosts, by the power of God, thrust down to hell Satan, and all wicked spirits who wander through the world for the ruin of souls".

AMEN.

AND GOD BE WITH THE RIGHT.

S

SORTS OF SCIENTISTS

CONFIRMED readers of *Candour* are well aware that political truths potentially capable of refuting officially generated lies are almost always terminated in the editorial womb so to speak; even if some honest, innocent author insists on giving birth to some true fact or candid comment, it will be the exception rather than the rule if it lives to be seen or heard some public day. This unmentioned censorship is literally a "fact of life" to which all media aspirants must accommodate their consciences or adopt some other profession.

But do would-be exponents of objective truth fare any better in other professions? Especially do they fare any better in the profession of science - the "new religion" freed from the dogmatic bonds of the Middle Ages when theology was Queen? Alas, the answer must be "No".

Nigel Balchin wrote a novel about *A Sort of Traitors* whom he saw as men of integrity who conceived it their duty - in pursuance of international peace - to convey, to unauthorised persons, the official secrets and expertise they were heirs to on account of their paid employment in their own countries atomic defence establishments. Balchin excuses their treason on the grounds of conscience: "the power to destroy the world should be shared by everyone", in the interests of liberty, equality, fraternity and peace pledges. The snag with this high-minded decision was that it had to be implemented clandestinely. National loyalty had to be abandoned in favour of loyalty to the international integrity of science - or words to that effect. We may think the novelist viewed this sort of traitor through fashionably red-coloured spectacles, perhaps he found the reality less sympathetic, or perhaps not. In the heyday of "exchange of nuclear information" (somewhat one-sided be it said) as some idealistic history-master said, "There can't be spies in peace time". So that was all right.

The ills of the Industrial Revolution were going to be cured by the universal application of nuclear power. International scientists would be the true saviours of the world: the leaders to send mankind on the way to the new hygienic peace and prosperity for all. The scientific bandwagon is crowded with theorists intent on solving the mysteries of the universe whilst justifying the expense accounts by providing the proletarian Jacks with all play and no work via the by-products of the time and space researchers. Pills and pesticides were freeing women from the kitchen sink, and men from the drudgery of digging. Theories abound whilst proofs are redundant.

Evolution has been with us so long now that even children in State kindergartens know that it is a fact, on account of the periodical croppings up of their rather oddly named ancestors: the Missing Links.

Only the other day, reported in *The Daily Telegraph*, there was an account of the latest "finds" in the Family Tree. This was Missing Link named, Ramidus, discovered in 1992 by Prof. Gen Suwa of Tokyo University, seems to have been represented by a "hominid tooth" described as "one of the oldest hominid teeth found", he is the ancestor of Australopithecus africanus, who was less chimpanzee-like than Australopithecus afarensis who preceeded him in the tale of evolution occupying untold millions of years. From this according to one, Dr. Asfaw, "the short cranial base and the hominid shapes of the canine and elbow (sic) show this species had already split from the apes - it had started to evolve toward human beings." So now you know. But as shown in the illustration (below) going forward a number of million years, there is no mention of Pithecanthropus, pictured in G.K. Chesterton's *Everlasting Man* in the '30s and designated, "The Portrait of a Thigh Bone."

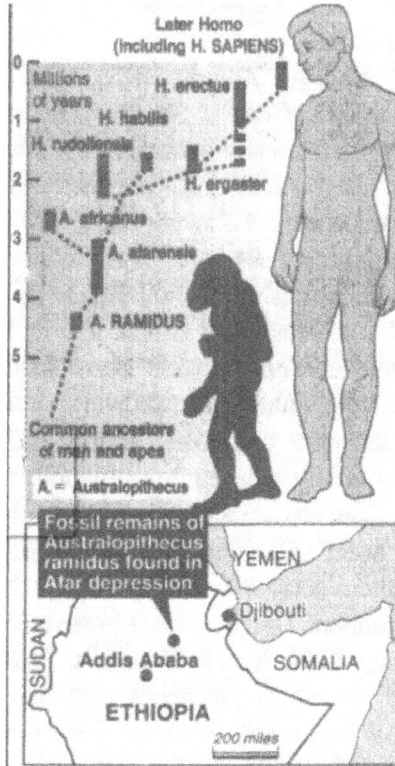

Also, there is no illustration of Archaeopteryx, the bird that evolved from a lizard, which has unobtrusively been removed from view in the British Museum. So what with this plethora of remains: "arms with no legs", "a molar tooth" and a thigh bone among the dust and ashes of millennia, there can be no doubts, according to the latest scientific team, in identifying the missing links as our ancestors, even though, "Without bones from the lower limbs, it is unable to tell if these primitive ancestors walked on two legs or four."

Nevertheless; "Scientists find Missing Link" is a headline guaranteed to establish or re-establish "the fact" of evolution in the minds of the most gullible people on earth, the media fodder.

SO WHAT ABOUT ANOTHER SACRED COW

Professor H. Dingle, who, alas, is now dead, wrote a book which he called *Science at the Crossroads*, after he had realised that there was what he considered to be a fatal flaw in Einstein's experiment concerned with the behaviour of clocks in certain circumstances which was - and is - considered definitive proof of the unassailable correctness of his Special Relativity Theory.

The Professor did not want to write the book as it did not show his scientific friends and/or colleagues in a very intelligent light. He wrote only after repeated questioning in private and public had failed to elicit a relevant answer let alone one that would show his criticism to be unfounded.

This is a cautionary tale of his experience in daring to question a theory which not only the author but the whole establishment accepts, presents and teaches as fact.

On the 19th August, 1970, the Reverend W.J. Platt formerly General Secretary of the British and Foreign Bible Society wrote to *The Times* saying:

"In *The Listener* last year there appeared a long correspondence following an article entitled *Definitions and Realities* by Professor H. Dingle, which was published on July 3rd. In its course certain alleged facts transpired which, if true, are manifestly of public concern. I have been waiting for some authoritative statement showing either that the assertions were unfounded or that steps were being taken to rectify a dangerous situation. As far as I am aware, none has appeared, and the implications of the matter seem so serious that public interest demands one without delay.

"Professor Dingle, who, I believe is recognised as a leading authority on Einstein's Special Relativity Theory, on which physicists acknowledge that they rely, has advanced what he claims to be a fatal criticism of that theory. On such a matter the layman is, of course, not qualified to speak; he is, however entitled to an assurance that the scientific world remains true to its principle of answering or accepting informed criticism. This appears to be not only, as it has always been, a moral duty of scientists, but, in these days, when the experiments performed are of such enormous potential danger, a necessity. According to the uncontradicted assertion in *The Listener* of October 30th last, however, the President of the Royal Society failed to give an assurance that scientific integrity is still preserved. If earlier statements in the correspondence are true, he could hardly, of course, do so."

"May I give a few of these statements?

1). Some of the most eminent workers in modern physics have admitted privately that they either do not understand the theory or regard it as nonsensical: nevertheless, they continue to teach it to students and to use it in high energy experiments.

2). It is stated that the Royal Society has declared privately that Professor Dingle's fallacy is: 'too elementary even to be instructive', but the Society has not stated what the fallacy is, and the journal *Nature* which had previously published the criticism without eliciting a refutation of it, has refused to publish a letter from Professor Dingle, asking that the Royal Society shall state the fallacy.

3). *New Scientist*, after asking Professor Dingle and Professor Synge, who I understand is an acknowledged mathematical authority on Relativity, the latter in a letter published in *Nature*, agreed that the point at issue was not an abstruse mathematical one but concerned only the possible behaviour of clocks, and Synge, cast his vote for Relativity. It is accepted that Relativity, which concerns itself with matters of space and time, must be dependent on measurement of time, i.e. on clocks. Dingle replied that the matter was not to be decided by voting and that his demand of one clock was that it should not work both faster and slower at the same time than another. This reply was not allowed publication in *Nature*, a fact which led two correspondents in *The Listener* to assume that Dingle had not replied.

The situation thus disclosed, if the facts are as stated, is alarming. According to Dingle's closing letter (Oct. 30th) all that is required to settle the matter is an answer to the question: What is it on Einstein's theory that determines which of the two clocks, relatively moving uniformly, lags behind the other, as Einstein says? Dingle's contention is that to be true, the theory demands that the clocks must work faster and slower at the same time! It is therefore untenable. I repeat, Sir, that I make no attempt to judge the issue, but ask, in the public interest, since the foregoing assertions have been published and remain uncontradicted, that an authoritative and conclusive assurance shall be given that scientific integrity continues to exist."

Dr. Platt received the reply from *The Times* that the letter was under consideration. As, several weeks later, it had not appeared and he heard nothing further, he wrote asking if a decision had been reached: he received no reply to the enquiry. The letter has not been published.

So Dr. W.J. Platt, was also subjected to "the silent treatment". But, one asks oneself - do such people forget the implications of this seemingly overwhelming press monopoly? One cannot complain of the "non-respectability" of such men as Dr. W.J. Platt and Professor Dingle, but the latter's book suffered much the same fate as the archaeopteryx, and disappeared from the booksellers' stocks as mysteriously as the 'missing link' from the British Museum.

And there the matter seems to have died with Professor Dingle until ten years on it was resurrected in *New Scientist* 7th August 1980 in an article entitled; *Why Pick on Einstein* by one Paul Davies, then a

Professor of Theoretical Physics at the University of Newcastle-upon-Tyne. In it he remarks upon "the scale and ferocity of the attack on the Theory of Relativity indicates "*a deep-rooted cultural antipathy*" (our italics) which does seem to show the peripheral presence of yet another shibboleth signifying persecution. Later on, he claims that "the late physicist Herbert Dingle enjoyed international notoriety, and acquired a retinue of adherents, largely on the basis of his attacks on the orthodox resolution of the 'twin-paradox' and... By making thought experiments sufficiently complicated, a wily anti-relativist can frequently bury an error amid a maze of observers, clocks and Rockets whizzing in various directions " Still there is no answer to the question posed by Professor Dingle in 1969, when he did not need to do anything controversial to gain recognition and adherents. He had them already; he fell into "the pool of silence" only because he posed an awkward question which presumably no one wanted to answer. When faced with this dilemma, he had been studying relativity for more than 50 years. He learned it in the first place, he says, from Professor A.N. Whitehead who "encouraged me in 1921 to write my first book on the subject (*On Relativity for All* - Methuen) and read the typescript of the book before it was published. During the following half century, I have studied intensively the field of investigation to which it belongs and discussed the theory with practically all those physicists whose names are best known in connection with it - Einstein, Eddington, Tolman, Whittaker, Schrodinger, Born, Bridgman, to name but a few. I knew some of them intimately. I worked for a year (1932-1933) with Tolman while he was writing his now standard work, *Relativity, Thermodynamics and Cosmology* (Clarendon Press) and he went through the m.s. with me and included in the book, what he called, "*Dingle's Formulas*" which I worked out for him, when, in 1940, I published my second book on the subject, (*The Special Theory of Relativity* - Methuen) now in its 4th edition and still much in use in universities in this country and in America.

Max Born wrote regarding it:

"I have enjoyed it very much, as your explanations of the difficult subject are very clear and well presented. I hope the book will find many readers."

When some twenty years ago, Whittaker who had direct firsthand knowledge of the origin of the theory, published his history of the whole field of thought of which Special Relativity forms a part now recognised as a standard work on the subject, I sent him some comments (on matters of substance, not mere typographical errors) to which he replied, 'many thanks for the corrections and comments. You have detected several mistakes which had been missed by my two proof collectors and myself: and some of the remarks and suggestions you make could have originated only from a vast background of knowledge, which fills me with admiration!' When the volume on Einstein in *The Library of Living Philosophers* (1949) was prepared, there were only two Englishmen among twenty five contributors selected from the world - I was one, the other has long been dead, so he could not have been one of the 'competent experts' whose judgement Sir Lawrence Bragg trusts. When Einstein died, I was summoned to broadcast a tribute to him on B.B.C. Television, which I did. Later Granada T.V. invited me to give a course on Relativity but by that time I was fairly well convinced that the Special Theory was untenable, so I refused. There are two articles on the subject in the *Encyclopaedia Britannica*, one by an American and the other by me. It was written before I had reason to reject the Special Theory, and when, recently, I was asked to revise it for the forthcoming new edition, I refused because I thought that my then unorthodox view made it undesirable for me to write, for a publication of that kind, the only article I could honestly write. The editor's, however, would not accept my refusal, but agreed to my writing on the subject as a controversial one and increased the length originally assigned." If any reader can name any scientist with equal or better qualifications than these who is willing to answer the question: "What is it in on Einstein's theory that determines which of the two clocks relatively moving uniformly, lags behind the other as Einstein says?"

We would be happy to hear from him, for until then it must be concluded that science is still at the crossroads and those who insist that any theory must be proved beyond question before it is taught as fact in the halls of learning, or indeed anywhere, will be on the outside looking in.

T

TRINITY OF TREASON

LAST month, as a memorial to Professor Revilo P. Oliver, we reprinted a quotation from his book, "*Christianity and the Survival of the West*", in which he concluded that the now almost ultimate success of "The homicidal conspiracy of Adam Weishaupt's Illuminati" against Christianity was owed, not so much to, "His subtle methods of deceit" as to "some fundamental weakness in his victims", i.e. the Christians of the white race.

We cannot find any reason to disagree with that diagnosis, so that if we are determined even at this late hour, to identify and succeed in curing the malignant disease that has brought the huge majority of Christians to apathetic - sometimes even enthusiastic - acceptance of each poisonous dosage that has rendered them progressively more resigned to their own demise, we must seek and find the antidote, and demonstrate its worth to any and every victim or assembly of victims whose attention we can command. So what precisely, has caused this "fundamental weakness?" In one word: "Heresy": defined as an opinion at variance with the defined truth; specifically, in religion, a heretic is one who adopts a contrary tenet of faith from those defined and accepted by the universal Christian Church which for sixteen centuries from the birth of Christ, Her Founder, was recognised wherever it was known in the world as the Church founded by Christ Himself, and the vessel of His Truth. Through those centuries, heresies and heretics came or went, periodically flourished or withered, but always outside the Church or in it but not of it, so to speak, until that fatal day when, on the death of that intimidating self-willed monarch, Henry VIII, Thomas Cranmer, Archbishop of

Canterbury, secret adherent of Martin Luther, felt free openly to deny the doctrine, known and defined as "Transubstantiation" i.e. the Real Presence, under the appearances of Bread and Wine of the Body and Blood of our Lord Jesus Christ in the Sacrament of the Altar, a fundamental tenet of the Christian faith: "Unless you eat of My Flesh and drink of My Blood, you will not have life in you." This heresy was different from all previous heresies in that it was made the reason for being of the "Church of England." And after that the deluge: Methodists, Congregationalists, Four Square Gospellers, Mormons, Christian Scientists *et al* The name is legion, as some other spirit said. The Catholics of England became martyrs, apostates, refugees, or just disappeared into latter-day catacombs. For nearly three hundred years "The Papists" as they were derisively known, were denied professional and/or independent status. Under pain of fine or imprisonment, they were forced into the Church of England or into exile. Enactments never removed from the Statute Book to this day. The Catholic Emancipation Act of 1829 freed them from those strictures however, and was followed by a brief national blossoming before the long decline when the service-going of members of the established Church became a minority habit, and then at last "The Smoke of Satan" entered and became visible in the Catholic Church. The pursuit of "Justice and Peace" and of "Liberation Theology" on Earth, became the preoccupation of the hierarchy, rather than the Way of the Cross and the attainment of the Kingdom of Heaven.

Divine Right took second place to human rights. Or it would be truer to say, since God was betrayed, Right turned into wrongs and the people found no one to redress them, so the Nation followed God into manufactured oblivion.

Thus the fruits of the second treason inevitably resulted in disillusionment engendering the physical and spiritual deterioration of peoples bludgeoned by the devastating wars and bloody tenor campaigns that made a shambles of Europe, and reduced the survivors everywhere to bewildered submissiveness, desperate for the transient peace and phoney justice offered by the fungoid growths mysteriously established on the political heights, promising a workers paradise where everyone would "give according to his capacity and receive according to his need."

But the socialist dilemma is basic: There must be no dissenters; only somehow, even with the strictest rule in the world, the Providence of the City of Man, unlike that of God, proved undisguisedly limited. This unpalatable fact has long been evident to even the most purblind of idealists, and yet, there must be no queues where everyone allegedly "receives according to his need." The logical solution presented itself with awful simplicity - dispose of the dissenters, thus drastically reducing the potential beneficiaries. But as was shown when mass murder was attempted on unprecedented scales via "World Wars" and "Terror" campaigns, so bloody a business became too unpopular long before its end was achieved (supposing it to be possible of achievement) since everyone is a dissident when his own life is the sacrifice demanded by an equalitarian creed that offers no reward but oblivion. Even in these decadent days, there are always too many people prepared to carry their crosses to Golgotha in the firm hope of bodily resurrection and the Beatific Vision, but not to Welwyn Garden City and the dubiety of a universal Welfare State. Another more acceptable route had to be discovered if the whole human race is ever to be herded into the limited pastures fertilised by the light of liberal humanism.

The route *has* been opened, and the last treason is under way. It remains to be seen if we are gullible enough to follow it. As if acting on the principle of what goes up must come down, the secret powers that drive us, having gone fruitlessly as far as they can with atheistic materialism, are now plunging heavily on theistic materialism to bring off the greatest confidence trick in history - or at least as great as The Old Serpent's tale about the "Tree of Knowledge." The pie in the ecclesiastical sky has been brought down to, an apparently more accessible, rice field in Bangladesh.

Everything is possible when "seeking first the Kingdom of God" if "God" is the Earth. Serving Gaia (feminism presumably calling for a Goddess) is made synonymous with "doing your own justice and peace" on Earth. Human Rights, Civil Rights, Equal Rights, indeed, any old Rights except Divine Right, however at odds their demands, serve to promote two essentials for the progress of Peoples toward the ultimate blasphemy of One World set to Rights by Man alone.

"WE HAVE NO KING BUT CAESAR"

If there is no Divine Right, there can be no Royal Right: (see Coronation Oath). Therefore Absolute Monarch is dead; the erstwhile subjects have no Sovereign; The Nation has no Sovereignty and no voice and thus can be killed in silence and buried in an unremarked grave.

The opening of this way to perdition has all the devilish ingenuity we usually associate with the complicated journey to the establishment of the One World Order prompted by the materialistic motive once roundly condemned, but now tacitly approved in "Christian Understanding" by Church leaders proclaiming the scandal of the neglected Rights of terrorists and subversives everywhere; "Brotherly Love" is expressed in ecclesiastic enthusiasm for mongrelising the Races: "The better to know you, my dear." Obedient Congregations, with lamentably few exceptions, seemingly have not noticed the fearsome irony of a Christianity that forgives the sinner whilst promoting the sins. The transformation of wrongs into rights is certainly a "Newer face of doom." "Be sure your sins will find you in the money" - even if it is borrowed money - appears among the modern aphorisms. "Love of the makers of money is the root of all riches", is evidently another.

When it comes to mass murder, how much less damaging to human sensibilities is the clinical efficiency of the abortion chamber. Instead of bloody heads falling into baskets in the Place de la Revolution, lives can be privately, though even more brutally, "terminated" with sterile efficiency. Dissident nurses can exercise their women's rights in the ranks of the unemployed. Or if that method of reducing the population should ever prove too crude to be reconciled with the New Christian Order, there is always the "conscientious right to prevent birth altogether - or if that is too chancy, what about sodomy and a change of sex if desired? All options are open to liberated Man - sorry, person.

It is clear that the Eternal Way, The Truth and The Life, as seen through the very latest dark glass, has imperceptibly become The Temporal Way, the comparative truth and death, without most of the progressing peoples noticing the sinister signs pointing to what endless desert the Rights road leads.

BUT TAKE HEART. IT IS STILL IMPERATIVE TO MAN THE BASTIONS.

The standard still is flying
Above the silent keep;
All battlements deserted
All sentinels asleep.

A shell of inlaid armour
Stands rusting by the throne.
The standard still is flying
But no-one is at home.

Our foes by invitation
Are now within the ward.
Below, the faithless minions
Prepare to serve the board.

Though Truth is long since murdered
And buried in the Fleet
It's always resurrecting
In field and farm and street.

Though public tongue and picture
Exert their alien powers,
Think shame to be defeated
While house-tops still are ours.

Unite and raise our voices
With one concerted shout,
Arouse a sovereign people
To drum all traitors out.

The standard still is flying,
So occupy the keep
Stand firm in the embrasures.
Let no man, faithless, sleep.

Put on that disused armour,
Stand by that ancient throne
Beneath the standard flying-
And sovereign be at home.

U

UNJUST WARS AND USURIOUS PEACE

HOWEVER difficult it may sometimes seem to decide whether any particular war is, or was, a just one; there is now no difficulty at all in knowing what is an unjust one. If, as has been said, "By their deeds you shall know them", we are presently confronted with the definitive evidence that the latest (twentieth century) comprehensive conflicts were "the unjustest" of them all; manufactured with the intention of ending all wars - especially just ones - in a universal slough of usurious peace.

The participants in those mutual massacres appear to be the very last of the dupes to realise that there never had been a "lady" in the pack for them to "find"; they and their fathers before them had been the victims of a gigantic con-trick from the beginning. Only today, in 1995, amidst the equally cynically organised celebrations for the "liberation" of the survivors of the alleged holocaust at Auschwitz in Poland and of the non-survivors (one hundred thousand or so) of the near obliteration of the 'open' city of Dresden in Germany in relentless raids by Lancaster bombers of the R.A.F. Only now, has it become almost undeniably obvious that the so-called Holocaust of the Jews was the non-existent "lady" that induced the deluded, devil-directed seemingly ill-assorted "allies" of empire and gulag to join, however reluctantly, the "liberating" armies called to do their "duty" in bringing about the horrors of the authentic holocausts of Hamburg, Dresden, Hiroshima and Nagasaki.

Yet, even now, there is no media mention, and certainly no contrition expressed, for the inexcusable and cold-blooded crimes committed by the manipulated hypocrites allegedly leading the self-designated United Nations, on the morrow of their triumph.

Nothing less than "unconditional surrender" having been demanded and, perforce, accepted, the whole population of Germany became prisoners of war; whereupon these righteous "war-to-end-war-peace-seekers" took thousands upon thousands of their "prisoners", herded them like cattle into fenced, guarded enclosures where they starved to death. This, under the auspices of the victorious Commander-in-Chief; the come-lately protégé of the "uncrowned king of the United States"; Bernard Mannes Baruch. General Dwight D. Eisenhower, soon to be rewarded with the Presidency of the United States under the same "uncrowned king".

The unsatiated victors, next handed back to their Soviet "allies", those million refugees who had escaped the Soviet gulag and joined the "forces of freedom". This under the management of Harold Macmillan of "wind of change" infame, afterwards ennobled Earl of Stockton; the millions duped were returned to their torturers to be murdered by order of Stalin - affectionately known in allied propaganda as "Uncle Joe".

General Mihailovich who fought for his King (Peter of Yugoslavia) and country (Serbia) was forced to fight an allied-armed communist usurper Tito. As soon as our "peace-seekers" laid hands on Mihailovich they hanged him for his patriotism.

So much for the Geneva convention.

After the rank and file, it was the turn of the German political and military hierarchy. The victors tried the vanquished for "war crimes"!!

We should not be surprised to learn that the legal proceedings at Nuremburg bore an uncanny resemblance to those of the High Priest's court in Jerusalem nearly two thousand years before, when Caiphas having heard only contradictory and unsatisfactory witnesses, and fearing an acquittal, exclaimed that they had no further need of witnesses and, disregarding the Jews' own law, declared the prisoner, Jesus of Nazareth, convicted out of his own mouth; which was just as illegal there as it would have been in a British Court in 1945. At Nuremburg, the witnesses were equally dubious, and they, the judges, advocates and jurors were all of the same "persecuted" race that the accused were charged with trying to exterminate; which did nothing to lend verisimilitude to the idea that what were being conducted at Nuremburg were "fair trials".

BRAVE AND DEDICATED

Two men who did all that they were able either to bring an end to the war and/or to avoid fighting for the wrong: William Joyce and Rudolf Hess provide the most cogent examples of the undeviating determination of our traditional enemy to stifle or strangle the truth no matter how illegal barbarous and scandalous the means.

William Joyce was an American who lived in England, loved her and loathed to see her being manoeuvred into declaring war on a Germany dedicated to the cause of defeating and destroying the atheist/communist empire ruled by Stalin. When he saw that the alien dominated Government at Westminster was going to be forced or bribed into such a declaration, with France reluctantly following, he determined to leave and go to Germany to pursue the same cause as before. He obtained the necessary passport by using a "terminological inexactitude"; (punishable at that time by a fine of thirty shillings); broadcast from Germany during the war, killed no one; was captured at its end; was brought to England; accused, charged, tried and convicted of treason and sentenced to be hanged by the neck until he was dead. He was brave and dedicated to the end regardless of the price to be paid. He gave up his life at peace with God and his conscience.

The story of Rudolf Hess has lately been partially recalled in the media on account of the vengeful vandalisation on private land of a privately created and owned memorial stone dedicated to him and his frustrated peace mission attempted in 1941.

He was at that time, Deputy Fuhrer of the Third Reich, and he flew from Germany to Scotland alone and unarmed. He landed safely and asked to meet the Duke of Hamilton with a view to enlisting his aid in persuading "the powers that were" at that time, i.e. Churchill, to consider a" peace process" but this now familiar play was not so popular among politicians it has since become. So he was immediately imprisoned incommunicado for the duration, and afterwards taken to and charged during the Nuremburg War Crimes Trials; found guilty and condemned to life imprisonment in Spandau, Berlin: that huge and gloomy fortress conveniently collectively under the control of the grandiosely termed "The Big Three", i.e. the U.S.A., Great Britain and the U.S.S.R., represented at the time by Roosevelt, Churchill and Stalin. There, Rudolf Hess was held in solitary confinement long after all others had been released on "humane" grounds.

When at last the fiction that Rudolf Hess could not have the same treatment because: "the Russians would not allow it" was exploded by Gorbachev, the impenitent man "who knew too much", and against all the odds continued to survive and remain mentally alert despite all that his gaolers dared to do, had to die before "the gaff was blown". So he did die: this 93 year old man who could not lift his arms above his head was alleged to have taken his own life by hanging himself with electric flex. If we can believe that, we can believe anything and there is no hope for us.

He was undoubtedly murdered, and to our national shame, it was the British who were in charge of security at Spandau at the time.

These brave men were neither the first, nor will they be the last to pay with their lives for daring to threaten the accomplishment of the aims of the Money Power.

May God give them "the peace that passeth understanding".

Which brings us to the usurious peace we now endure.

The moneylenders create the only currency and thus reign supreme. The European empires have been eaten away from within; chaos abounds in these erstwhile ordered lands, the betrayed indigents of the Caribbean, India, Pakistan et al, encouraged and financed by the you know who's, arrived Establishment aided and welcomed, first in England and Wales, "to enable the National Health Service to operate", (Enoch Powell); they were followed by members of every disparate race who could afford a dubious passport, marry a British citizen, smuggle aboard the equivalent of a banana boat or be ferried across the Channel by promoters of the immigration industry. Now, of course, anyone can come through Europe and become a pampered part of the ethnic minority in no time. The difficulty for the English is to discover the whereabouts of any compatible majority community for them. The immigration industry remains one of the few flourishing enterprises left to us. No coal, no fish, (wasn't it Aneurin Bevan who said, "we walk on coal and we are surrounded by fish and it would take an administrative genius to provide a shortage of either"). Debt-ridden farmers - prisoners of the payments on the mammoth machines that have put both men and animals out of work and turned the countryside into pest and chemical infested prairies without hedges or character. Poor Merrie England; no villages - only "estates" filled with commuters; no country towns; only parking lots, supermarkets and chain stores.

The surrounding countryside is in danger of being trampled underfoot by the home bred tourists whose "rights" no landlord may gainsay, unless he happens to be an Arab or a Jew in the privileged classes: i.e.

they are rich. And the cities, what of them? Ask the dispossessed whose homes were demolished to make way for a coffee-coloured-elephant called Canary Wharf - and the rest of the flattened East End? Is that what we fought for - "England home and beauty? G.K. Chesterton once said no man ever fought for anything else.

And it was all stolen by the new, unhappy lords, who know no songs.

V

VIRUS IN THE VATICAN

THERE is undoubtedly "something rotten in the State" of the Vatican, but Catholic Church inmates, ex-mates, enemies and on-lookers all seem very much at variance in their ideas and estimates of what, when and how the apparently healthy body found itself suddenly a helpless prey to the latest religious virus: variations of latter-day Gnosticism.

Anyone who has read Mary Martinez's block-busting book: *The Undermining of the Catholic Church* can be under no delusion that "it is nothing to worry about" or that "it all began" (like a post W.W.1 influenza epidemic) in the wake of the Second Vatican Council; but still, as in politics, it was the gradualness of the erosion over the decades, of what had been thought to be inviolate doctrine, that caused the bewildered confusion among clergy and congregations everywhere until the great majority of sheep obeyed their herd instinct and stayed where they were seeking what sustenance is still available in the eroded pastures. It was the shepherds who were "scattered".

There is always a snake in the tree, waiting to advocate the digestion of "knowledge" as indispensible for the acquisition of the superior understanding which, transcending faith, will enable the man who gains it to reach equality with, even transcendence of his creator. How ironic it is that these latest new age-one worlders whilst telling themselves and less gifted mortals, that they are now on the verge of completing the improving changes to the original Divine creation suggested by their own unaided reasoning powers, should have fallen for the wiles of the world's first confidence trickster and his long "busted flush"; for all their self-vaunted superior intelligence, they can only come up with an equally unoriginal version of the Gnosticism that saw our first progenitors out of Eden.

Addis and Arnold's *Catholic Dictionary* is very revealing on the subject of the turning of Gnosticism (higher knowledge) into "the formal principle of heresy".

It says: "Let the allegorical interpretation be applied to the New Testament, and let its literal sense be put aside as worthless, and then, under the plea of higher knowledge, Christianity might be changed at will. A man had but to suppose himself possessed of this higher gift, and then, on a plea of allegorizing he might explain away every fact and doctrine in the traditional belief. Nor need he trouble himself about explaining it away. He might mutilate the text of the gospels: he might mix tenets borrowed from the heathen philosophy or religions with Christianity; he might by treating the moral law as he had treated Christian doctrine, invent a new code of ethics. All this he might do, and all this the Gnostics actually did. In fact, when the way was opened, the motives for pressing into it were strong enough."

Thus: the definition. Then came the punch lines: the results of its adoption.

"The age of the Gnostics was eager for novelties in religion, and addicted to fantastic superstitions. It was the fashion of the time to mingle philosophy, mythology and magic. There was then more inducement to amend Christianity by the introduction of foreign elements, because, whilst it showed a life and power to which neither philosophy nor heathenism could pretend, its teaching on creation out of nothing, on the resurrection of the body, on salvation through the sufferings and death of Christ the Son of God, ran counter to every prejudice of the heathen world. There was not a sect among all the countless sects of Gnosticism which did not deny each one of these doctrines. Above all, the central idea of Gnosticism made it welcome to many who were half-converted from heathenism." (Or today: to many who are half-reconverted to it.)

"It was a knowledge superior to and independent of faith. Faith was for the multitude", - the opium of the masses? - "knowledge for the few".

"Such then, was the nature of Gnosticism. It was a false knowledge which threw off the trammels of faith and ecclesiastical authority. It subjected everything to the caprice of the individual," (freedom of conscience) "and made any fixed rule of faith impossible." Easily recognisable as Satan's sin: pride. But he is Lucifer who was the brightest one in Heaven where every creature sees God who made him, so the fall of Satan and his followers was irredeemable. So, the human race became the target of the fallen angels' irreversible malice and of God's redeeming grace.

In what then, do our "modernists" differ from those who "professed to impart a knowledge greater and deeper than the ordinary doctrine of Christians, knowledge which forgot the limits of reason and scorned to believe what it could not understand?"

Well, they certainly no longer boggle at believing "what else they do not understand", if evolutionists provide any comparison.

Again, as in the beginning of the second century A.D., it is important to remember in the ending of the twentieth that Gnosticism is not a philosophy although it is as "unfettered and unstable as any philosophy could be," now as then, it keeps a semblance of Christianity for without its Christian elements it could not be in a position of dialogue - that fashionable phrase - with the Catholic Church. The prelates of the Church could not prattle about "seeking the good in every religion," from snake charmers to voodoo practitioners.

However, the really fundamental difference between Gnosticism then and Gnosticism - or modernism - now is not just the arrogance of the "intellectuals" such as Teilhard de Chardin or Hans Kung but the obduracy of the hierarchy in flouting the Syllabus of Errors, no longer insisting on the taking of the anti-modernist oath before ordination to the priesthood and the abandoning of the Mass of all time for the priest and "People of God," to enjoy a convivial "meal" preferably to the accompaniment of a "pop" band, hopefully "to entice the young". Knowledge (Gnosticism) in this democratic age is not just for "the few" it is for "the many". What was the Bolshevik phrase? "The opium of the people"? So we are back to the errors of Soviet Russia "which will spread all over the world if we do not heed the exhortation of the Mother of God at Fatima to: Pray for the conversion of Russia that the Pope will dedicate that unfortunate country to her Immaculate Heart, which, if done in conjunction with all the bishops of the Catholic Church will bring about "peace for a time".

The "people", some of them, have prayed and "a Pope" has dedicated, since 1917 when the request was made, but somehow there were fewer mentions of Russia before the prayers, and the dedication when at last it was made, was not pronounced in conjunction with all the bishops and "Russia" was attached parenthetically with "the world". So - no conversion and the reverse of peace anywhere. The papal leadership is now conspicuous for its ambiguity and the virus in the Vatican looks to be in the bone which makes it incurable except by a miracle. But will God perform that necessary miracle since mankind has so signally failed to act upon the warnings although accompanied by apparitions at La Salette and Fatima of the Queen of Heaven herself climaxing in the "miracle of the sun" witnessed by thousands of people, not a few of them atheists or sceptics in no mood to be fooled, who could only fall on their faces in terror at what seemed like the beginning of the end of the world.

Now that Modernism in the Church is the rule rather than the exception, the relaxations of men appear to have superseded the Commandments of God.

Euphemisms soften the erstwhile unequivocal description of sexual sins. Fornication becomes "having a relationship"; adultery: "having an affair"; contraception: "family planning"; abortion: "termination of pregnancy"; and lastly: the sins crying out to heaven for vengeance: wilful murder; the sin of sodomy; oppression of the poor; defrauding labourers of their wages. How often do we hear the sins of abortion and contraception related to the first; statements from the pulpit relating the "gay scene" to the second and usury to the third and fourth? In fact sin is seldom mentioned at all. It is all brotherly love, even if it does sometimes look suspiciously like temptation to commit sodomy; and as for hell fire that is just a medieval bogey to elicit funds for the grasping princes of the Church.

Since we know that God will not do for us what we can very well do for ourselves; we have to understand at last that the prideful, erstwhile "few" have so spread "their" fatal disease that they have become the stupid "many". It is now we who are "the few"; we who possess the "knowledge" to do the will of the everlasting God who will give us strength to bring to battle and defeat "the many" in this final conflict.

W

WASTE AND WELFARE

HOWEVER beneficial later generations thought the conquest of England in 1066 was to the development of people and country, the contemporary inhabitants heartily agreed with their chosen Leader/King, Harold Godwinson, that "not one foot of English ground" should be yielded to invaders if he and his army could prevent it. They denied any right of the Norman-nourished Edward-the-Confessor - Saint or no - to bequeath *their* country to "The Bastard of Falaise", the then Duke of Normandy. They followed Harold enthusiastically to victory at Stamford Bridge over Harold Hardrada, the invading King of Norway then in cahoots with Harold's traitor brother, Tostig. In that desperate battle both were killed But there was no time for celebration, no sooner had Harold re-occupied the city of York than he was apprised of the landing in Pevensey Bay of the Duke of Normandy and his marauding army. With no time for rest and recuperation the victors of Stamford Bridge began their punishing march south, through London, to pick up the Kentish Fyrd - Militia, to us - to Hastings to do battle with the Norman "Freebooters" as they termed them, before they could advance further from the beaches on which they had landed.

Harold and his Housecarls[19] died to a man on the hill the Normans named Senlac (Lake of Blood), and the over enthusiastic Fyrd, whose optimistic indiscipline contributed largely to the defeat, were slain or scattered, and the conquest was on its way. Since, as we know, victors write history, students today are seldom encouraged to make a study of the immediate and long term equivocal results of that defeat.

---

[19] Effectively the Saxon professional soldiers and household troops.

In 1066 however, "the people and the country" were as helpless and hopeless as orphans of the storm. All resistance was crushed without mercy - in the process Yorkshire and half Mercia were laid waste. The English became the "lower classes" in what had been their own land - remind you of anything? - the game laws took whole forests away from the people and then more acres to create new ones for their conquerors to hunt in. Normans were the lords of the Marches and in the decades after the conquest built and occupied huge castles and became the first power in the land between the King and the people in the feudal system. Since the "Knights" that "came over with the conqueror" were for the most part fortune hunters, it follows that they expected rewards which had perforce to come from the Saxon noblemen's property. Thus, Lords and Peasants were both deprived. Stories of real heroes such as Hereward the Wake and fiction and fable such as Ivanhoe and Robin Hood show how long and deep was the resentment. The Norman acquisitive ambitions did not stop there. Since there were no longer any "Royals" or Peers in the local marriage mart, the Norman overlords looked to France for dowered brides. Anjou, Aquitaine, Provence and more came into the conquering Norman possession to engender centuries of family feuds, dynastic wars and defensive and offensive conflicts to sap the strength and substance of passive England. Then there was the Duchy to be administered and defended against the annexing ambitions of the Kings of France. England, in fact became the Conqueror's base camp whilst he dealt with a rebellious son (Robert in Normandy), wars against Scotland, Wales and France. His sons Robert and William (Rufus) inherited respectively the Duchy of Normandy and the Kingdom of England, but the warfare continued. Nobody loved William II; incompetent in war, perfidious in peace - the short times there was any peace - he was murdered at last by "person or persons unknown", and Henry, the Conqueror's only English born son was elected King by the Witan (the Anglo-Saxon National Council).

England had a legitimate, English-born King again; the first since Harold.

LADY OF ENGLAND

Henry I restored by charter the abrogated laws of the Confessor and the Conqueror; recalled the Archbishop of Canterbury who had been banished by William II so that he might seize the English Church revenues. There were also popular reforms in the administration of justice and an also popular marriage with Matilda, daughter of Malcolm of Scotland, who was descended from the ancient Royal House. Even so, the waste went on. Henry made war on his brother Robert's badly governed Duchy and the French King who coveted it. Although Henry put down the Normandy rebellion and defeated the French, there was only a pause in the seemingly endless wasting wars.

Henry's only legitimate son was drowned when returning from Normandy to England. Henry himself died in France after having made his Barons in England swear to receive his daughter, Matilda as Lady of England. Peaceful succession was not to be; the Crown was seized by Henry's nephew, Stephen of Blois. Civil war ensued. Matilda being married to Geoffrey Plantagenet, son of the Count of Anjou, her son thus became Duke of Normandy and Count of Anjou and on the death of Stephen became Henry II, King of England. *He* married Eleanor of Aquitaine and through her added a couple more pieces of France to his Dominions (Poitou and Guienne) which, of course, necessitated more wars to defend them.

From then on, the Angevin Royals quarrelled incessantly among themselves, with their in-laws, and since by then they were related to half of France and had matrimonial ties with Scotland and were jealous of any they considered upstart chieftains in Ireland and Wales, there was always some military drain on the Royal revenues, so it was no wonder that the Church property was seized periodically along with the people's.

That was why Thomas, Archbishop of Canterbury was murdered - in defence of the Realm - though few students realise it now. The Angevin vaunting ambition and obsession with their continental inheritances had resulted in two centuries of wasteful wars with more to come. It is now perhaps difficult for twentieth century students to understand the native enthusiasm for Richard I, called The Lionheart; that may be because of his portrayal as a violent persecutor of the Jews. What perusal of English history does not show the picture of Richard riding, sword in hand belabouring poor defenceless Hebrews in city streets? His subjects, however, much preferred their King to demand contribution from the Jews to finance the Third Crusade to his predecessor's habit of milching the coffers of both State and Church to finance fruitless war on all their neighbours. When Richard was captured and held prisoner in Austria on his way back from the Holy Land, his subjects contributed to his ransom and welcomed him back with enthusiasm. Having suffered nearly a decade of his would-be usurping brother's depredations; but still, as G.K. Chesterton wrote sometime later, the people of England did not speak. Richard died. John reigned. More unrewarding war. More waste.

The Church and the Barons forced the Monarch to sign the Great Charter which incorporated the Common Law of England. But still the wars went on. Scotland and France continued as hereditary enemies. Thus the "Middle Ages".

ENGLAND IS LAID WASTE

When the devastation occasioned by the twentieth century wars is considered, it makes two or three hundred years of almost perpetual warfare from the eleventh to the fourteenth century seem "No such great matter". The difference however is not just the degree of destruction but in the reasons, *why*? Our European mediaeval ancestors were no more venal or virtuous than any of their predecessors or descendants but they did not adopt any highminded, do-gooding reasons for their aggression such as uniting to bring about world - or even local - peace. They followed their leaders either because "some foreigner" was trying to take what was theirs or because it was their feudal duty. The frequency of conflict was only possible because being members of mainly agrarian societies, "the other ranks" were only available after the sowing and before the harvest, and there was no provender in the winter countrysides. The Normans having established the Feudal system in England, the "Call to Arms" was the equivalent of Income Tax only it was paid in kind. Because of our modern obsession with money, it is easy to forget that money has no value except as a means to facilitate the exchange of goods or property.

Thus, mediaeval war wasted only life and time, property merely changed hands which probably accounts for the frequency of attempts by the losers to win it back again or the winners to increase their holdings; anyway the land remained and was rarely neglected. Wars were fought to a pattern and left no debts until (as we were reminded recently by a *Candour* correspondent) the odd Popes and Kings who should have known better "went to the Jews" who had for untold centuries understood very well that the "means of exchange" could also be a "means of irreversible transfer" if handled correctly and incessantly by gullible *goyim* who gave their birthright for it and are seemingly too stupid to think themselves accursed for having done so.

Now all England is laid waste and we "disinherited" with the ruins all about us, are told by the barbarians who purport to rule us that we are tenants in a welfare state of their making which is open to anyone who cares to come and occupy the property, and that it is our bounden duty to welcome them into the parlour and cheerfully give up the best bedroom whilst continuing to be responsible for the payment of rent and taxes plus the National Debt. All in the interests of world peace you understand.

ANYONE FOR THE CRUSADE?

CRY GOD FOR ENGLAND AND ST. GEORGE!

X

FOR some people, X marks the spot: for others it is an algebraic symbol; and to nearly everybody, at some time or other, X is "the unknown quantity" and if we ever needed to know certainly and unforgettably, who and what, politically and economically speaking, is that quantity, it is now.

The front page of *The Independent* newspaper of 17th May, 1995, carried a banner headline: "Labour Promises to Reform the Bank of England"... Just to make sure everyone is reminded that electioneering is in the air; promises such as this abound at such times, both from the Party that is threatened and the Party that threatens with loss or gain of the position of Party in power for the next five years following the exercise of the "democratic people's right to vote." When the time comes for the various candidates for election to Parliament to confront their potential supporters from the platforms provided by the rates - paid local councils and bespoke T.V. screens, one would take the longest odds offered in a wager that the character the "reformed" Bank of England will assume when and if the "reformation" takes place, will not have anything to do with the removal of the power and monopoly of the said bank to create interest-bearing I.O.U's masquerading as legitimate currency and passed to the government of the day to be fraudulently lent to the public at interest whilst gulling them into thinking they have been provided with a free means of exchange for goods and services. Supposing that this particular election promise will not be lost in the welter of victory or defeat, as is the fate of so many promises of the past, the only outcome is likely to be a transfer of the actual issue to some "United Europe" set-up, or a crooked by-pass to an even more deleteriously "reformed" world bank, whose creators, directors and the unnatural heirs thereof will be as much of an unknown quantity as ever the originals were.

Conspiracy buffs such as ourselves had no sooner acquired, assimilated and broadcast to our necessarily limited capacity, the knowledge of, and seeming transcendancy of one Bernard Baruch, a stocks gambler on Wall Street who became a billionaire in the twenties whilst less perspicacious "players of the market" were - in the graphic phrase of an Italian/American - "falling out of Wall Street windows like confetti" than his ascendancy seemed to be attracting satellites even, perhaps rivals in other hemispheres. Even so, "Bernie" in his own sphere, became, in the nature of a society where the dollar was king, the "advisor" to five successive presidents and was journalistically designated, "The uncrowned king of the United States" - "The king of kings" so to speak, which was quite as blasphemous as it sounds. Later, he was the benevolent host of the "Out of office and favour" and thus impoverished, Winston Churchill, when that greedy gambler, was on a fortune hunt in New York. "Winnie seems to have hit the jackpot that time, being salvaged after a traffic accident in the vicinity of Baruch's New York residence, and entertained (if that is the word) by "the uncrowned king" whilst "convalescing". Not surprisingly this unpublicised and seemingly fortuitous acquaintanceship proved to be the foundation of the financial Churchill summitry, and the penthouse goal of the Baruchian political elevator. "The greatest living Englishman" attained his title by co-operation with two other Baruch "subjects": Franklin D. Roosevelt, contemporary President of the United States of America and Dwight D. Eisenhower, the tyro General placed in supreme command of allied forces in "winning the war" as a necessary prelude to their overlord Baruch's post hostilities arrival in Britain to announce that he had come, in his own words, "to wave the big stick over the big boys to see that they don't foul up the peace." (Perhaps it was not a coincidence that the code word for the 1945 cross channel invasion was "Overlord"). Now that they are all dead with their glamourised reputations more or less intact in the teeth of the enduring results of the un-fouled "peace", can we doubt that that same "peace" was agreed to, though not organised by the Baruch political minions?

Still that leaves "The once and future "(financial) kings" whose uncrowned heads pop up with monotonous regularity in national and international courts, securely screened from public awareness by the "palace" servants from major-domos to scullery maids - appropriately located in the House of Commons and/or Representatives on either side of the Atlantic.

There is nothing new in all this: the play is age old, and there seems never to have been any lack of suitable candidates to play either major or minor roles in each revival, (slightly amended) performance. The spotlights are set to illuminate selected "stars" on the world stage for as long as the current strategy calls for it, but how rarely do we catch a glimpse of the "backer of the production" or, as G.K. Chesterton once said... even more importantly, "the bankers of the backers". Even when we do, the roles are sometimes combined to make confusion worse confounded. Rothschilds. Rockefellers, Warburgs and such, abound but Pattersons, Kuhns, Loebs, Brown Shipley and all, are almost never to be seen in prominent positions either on the stage or in the box seats during performances, especially when "the big scene" is on.

CAPITULATION

When Anthony Eden was doing his "Go-Stop" part over Suez in 1956, it was only when Field-Marshal Montgomery was given the necessary job of explaining to a group of army officers why the already successful re-occupation of the Canal Zone campaign was reversed, that anyone learned of the order relayed by Dwight Eisenhower, President of the United States, for the troops to be withdrawn under pain of economic sanctions if the order was not obeyed forthwith. One of the officers at that meeting considered it his patriotic duty to make public that capitulation on the part of the Prime Minister of Great Britain to what can only be described as an ultimatum relayed by the President of the U.S.A., Britain's supposed ally[20]. We still do not know which particular backer or banker ordered Eisenhower in so peremptory a fashion that the telephone call was initiated from Washington at eight o' clock in the evening so that poor puppet Eden was hammered at 2 a.m. G.M.T. No wonder he retired with a nervous breakdown after being confronted whilst addressing Young Conservatives from the platform in the Festival Hall, London, by a member of the League of Empire Loyalists who asked him, "How many more times are you going to scuttle from Suez?" The hall was packed with Y.C.s because it was their annual conference. But, needless now to say, there was no demand for an answer from even one of those brainwashed apprentices in party politics. The only outcome was howls of execration from those present and a media rebuttal as far as the content of the question was concerned. As the scene had been performed before television cameras, there were, of course, thousands of viewers but as most people have poor memories for the spoken word and not much will to read more of the newspapers than the headlines, Mr. Eden was speedily removed from office and the next phase could proceed under the blanket of the media dark.

The next disappearing from empire act was Cyprus: for that there had to be an exacerbated problem for which the only cure would be British withdrawal from the country and the bases which only months before had been declared such excellent substitutes for Suez that we

---

[20] The officer reported it to A.K. Chesterton, then editor of *Candour*, disregarding the Official Secrets Act as it was a case of treason - it was duly published in *Candour* and as duly ignored by the media.

would "probably have left the canal anyway." So, as soon as the public were judged to have forgotten the millions of pounds worth of equipment abandoned in the zone, "The problem" manifested itself in demands for union with Greece on one side and freedom from oppression on the other. Again, we do not know precisely who the stage manager was or by whom appointed but the cast was on the stage and "rarin' to go"; Greek Cypriots calling for "enosis" (union with Greece): the Turkish minority demanding partition. Firearms and bombs were stored in the Orthodox Archbishop's palace in Nicosia. the Turks came down like wolves on the fold to help their Cypriot brothers as soon as they understood the ruling power had abdicated and the British troops found themselves in the situation before and since made so familiar, in Palestine and Ireland: "be killed rather than kill". Thence to negotiations; Archbishop Makarios to England and the result as predictable as all the other peace-meals that decimated an empire on which the sun had been ordered to set.

Still we do not know which particular financial or political tool was in the manipulation of the unknown overlord. But we can provide a list of likely organisations runners and riders which may help some of us to "read the form" and pick the favourite, if not the winner, who is likely to be a late entry anyway. Though because of the number of unpredictables, it is not "a betting race" as the pundits say.

We will treat it as a unique stage managed race and save ourselves from the mixed metaphor.

THE CAPITAL X WE THINK HAS NOT YET MADE HIS ENTRANCE.

Y

YOUTHANASIA

THE malignancy of the policy adopted by the world governors-in-waiting is intended to ensure, come the millennium, when it is predicted that the messianic (Jewish) race will begin its reign, that the population will be so disorientated as to be reduced to irreversible subservience.

This, as all other policies of the same ambitious race, began its effect when the first cash payment was made to the first Christian traitor, Judas Iscariot, and has continued ever since, with fluctuating fortunes, in all climes and times until today, when the advent of the desired supremacy is being media-plugged by the apostles of Satan all day and every day with increasing arrogance. The arrival of the anti-Christ is being anticipated anytime between 1996 and the end of the century. So now we know, or do we?

The media, which presently are the conglomerate substitute for "the voice crying in the wilderness", seem quite as certain as was St. John the Baptist, that the day of fulfilment is at hand. The "national" press, "B."B.C. and "Independent" Television abound with news reports and items, debates, articles and comment on every aspect of the coming world unity, all of which seems to have been, and to be, accepted as "inevitable" by probably 96% of the population of the British Isles, although without any sign of enthusiasm; that is left to the 2% suborners and suborned to express. We, Right rebels, are the heirs to the ever recalcitrant 2% who, to the self-appointed master racials fury, are "like the poor, always with us."

The apathy is, of course, just what the messianic racists have ordered, and will order until the ultimate X arrives.

Whilst it has taken the perfidious Jews nearly two thousand years to reach what they obviously think is the last lap on their journey to mastery of the world, it would take only seconds for straying-should-be Christians to turn to the Right road if they only ask for direction from the Creator of the world and follow his Redeemer Son who has travelled the way through suffering and death, to clear the blocks that vandals have erected on destructive expeditions down the ages. The Risen Christ has made the way passable for anyone with the grace and perseverance to plod through the dust and clamber over or around the obstacles malevolently reared. But it is not enough for us just to save ourselves; charity as well as common sense demands that we should stay to help our blinded neighbours to regain, at least, the *will* to be led by those who can still see, even though it is "Through a glass darkly." The blind are thus because they have been dosed from infancy with sugar-coated poison which has so impaired their mental vision that they are incapable of seeing the signposts, let alone reading them, and so, will continue to follow the seemingly pleasant path they have been told will go on forever even when the scenery becomes increasingly less inviting than forecast. There have been periods and places when clarity of sight and thought were sufficiently widespread for those times to be viewed nostalgically by later generations as ages of Faith. But it is now so long since there was one of those, that hardly anyone under seventy years of age has been told the truth of their existence and if one were now told, so deliberately distorted are the present day ideas of what is good or beautiful, he would find it hard to believe that such a way of life was history and not some do-gooder's dream - except that it was much too commonsensical to appeal to worshippers of Earth goddesses and such - besides the people were said to be merry!

With sixteenth century decimation of Christendom: the seventeenth century re-establishment of the hierarchy of usurers in England, followed by the eighteenth century rationalism, Europe staggered from one wrong road to another but still with tiny minorities clinging to the ancient faith, some of whom left their native lands to establish themselves in what they hoped would be new Englands, Frances, Netherlands or Germanies; where, leading pioneering lives in alien continents they spread their social, but not necessarily their religious cultures, worldwide. British, French, Dutch and Germans fought (often among themselves) for "Living space", converted or dominated and - especially in the case of the British in America - shook off the trammels of their countries of origin and thought themselves free... only to discover, as others before them, that the power of money is international and the love of it breeds internationalists.

So: first fell royal rule. The "sins of the fathers" - and brother, were visited with a vengeance upon Richard III, the last of the Plantagenet's. The feckless fornication and lust for land of Edward IV, Edward III and John of Gaunt spawned the bastard offspring that sparked rebellion, usurpation and finally recourse to usurers who thus have since mastered every monarch in England except Charles II.

The Royals were over-ruled either by their own passions or the greed for money that only usurers agreed to satisfy - at their own price: the crack of Christendom released the hoards of heresy, with us to this day; only the Catholic Church by the Grace and Will of God still stood, as now it does - but with how tattered a robe!

INDUSTRIAL REVOLUTION

Neither the first nor the second Elizabethans have ever admitted (if they realised it) that through that fatal loss of sovereignty came all the subsequent ills our political flesh is heir to.

Since neither regicide nor religious persecution, treason nor usurpation aroused the contemporary people of England, "who have not spoken yet", to effective protest, we need not wonder at the present evident almost universal indifference in the face of the undisguised advance of what are trained overwhelming forces prepared for D-Day in the Third (and our enemy hopes) last World War; it has been schemed, crafted and recruited over centuries. As Roosevelt's classic phrase has it "Things do not just happen, they are planned that way." The latest phase of the planned apathy began with "The emancipation of women." (So downtrodden in the Middle Ages that they took over their husbands castles and estates and managed them to profit whenever their spouses went on crusade). Twentieth century wives were still given to finding devious ways of influencing the political actions of their husbands; they also still considered it their duty to bring up their children in the traditional ways they should go (even if it was accomplished via the "nanny"); it was not only the so-called upper classes who were exhorted to be bound by "Noblesse Oblige"; craftsmen and peasants had had their own immemorial standards too.

All this had to go.

The Industrial Revolution the Victorians were so proud of began the demise of craft apprenticeships; Enclosure Acts left the dispossessed peasants and few acre farmers nowhere to go but to the assembly lines, the soulless streets or the city slums. Death duties combined with wholesale military slaughter destroyed what was left of the landed gentry and paid parliamentarians completed the subordination of "The Commons" to the diktat of alien bankers. However, whilst families were still close knit in faithful union, it proved impossible to impose an alien culture on a people with no vacuum in their souls.

So: if the apostles of Satan were going to complete the second Fall of Adam and Eve by the prophesied time, how much simpler to tempt the children with the sweets of their desiring, having made them vulnerable by separating their natural guardians - their parents.

"They" looked upon it, and saw the strategy was good. Its implementation was soon given ("Nothing happens by chance") an unprecedented boost:- The Great War!

The carnage of the trenches on the Western Front called for the back-up of every patriotic woman, especially the selfless wives and sisters who volunteered in their thousands to nurse the wounded at home and overseas; to drive ambulances; to "man" assembly lines in ammunition factories and to serve on farms, fields and in offices or wherever the shortage of men left vacancies. When there were no more volunteers, both sexes were conscripted.

Death, separation, disablement and "liberation" destroyed "the family" as an "immovable object."

Come the "peace": The loss of a million or more potential breadwinners, and the inadequacy of compensation forced widowed mothers to seek work in the labour market; the emancipated factory workers no longer saw themselves as "Daughters living at home" subject to parental authority until marriage; especially as nearly a whole generation of potential mates had died in the Flanders mud, drowned in the cruel seas or become disabled pensioners for life.

The hardships of separation, the rigours of war and the post-war miseries of homelessness, poverty and incompatibility were too much for the weakest to bear and the bespoke legislators were only too anxious to "help" with "dole", divorce, "National" Insurance and other sops to allay the hopeless depression on the scrap heap still awaiting transformation into the promised "land fit for heroes to live in."

Thereafter; contraception, abortion, "planned" pregnancies, artificial insemination, fornication, adultery and finally rampant sodomy served to promote the post-Christian communities that are sometimes still lauded as the beneficiaries of brilliant mankind's success in building a better world where everyone is equal... well...did someone say "some are more equal than others"?

FORCES OF EVIL

In 1931, before that nadir was reached, not only Great Britain but her whole empire were in such a parlous condition that desperate political figureheads were forced to justify their positions somehow, so they agreed to call an Imperial Conference at which in 1932, the mother country, her dominions and colonies agreed to trade with one another on advantageous terms. The system was called Imperial Preference. In 1933, Adolf Hitler became Chancellor of the Third Reich; Benito Mussolini was earning Churchillian bouquets for the rejuvenation of Italy; both would be in Axis alliance and agreeing trading preferences with Japan. So what would poor usurers do then? "They" knew, if no one else did.

By 1939, what a different story: Hitler was a monster who was to kill all the Jews in Germany; Mussolini was a clown whose best achievement was, "To make the trains run on time", and Japan, who had been Britain's ally in the Great War, was now a "Yellow Peril". Weirdest of all, Josef Stalin; the murderer, enslaver of tens of millions of Soviet citizens and rapist of Finland was overnight lined up to be transposed into a friend and ally who must be protected at any cost.

No need to repeat what the outcome of all that was - we live with it.

In the 1930's, just when it seemed that the nations were on the verge of freeing themselves from the thrall of the Jewish Money Power, that power's secret weapon burst upon an obediently horrified world - The Holocaust, which we now know was in embryo in 1919[21], appeared in the middle of Europe, apparently fostered by Hitler himself and now released like a fully grown gorgon ready to gobble up all the Jews in

---

[21] See *Candour*, February 1995.

Germany unless its vile master and his ferocious people were stopped before the victims were eaten alive... or words to that effect. So: Great Britain and her empire, France, Belgium, The Soviet Union, Chiang Kai-Shek's China and the United States of America all went to war (some later than others) with the German nation, the Italian nation and the Japanese nation...

POOR CHILDREN

1995 being the 50th anniversary of the so-called United Nations' great victory over the "Forces of evil", the event was celebrated by the veterans of the campaign who - on television at least - appeared to be vastly outnumbered by the weeping survivors of the Holocaust.

And where was the youth in all this celebration of the world having been made safe for democracy? What were the heirs to the spoils of the victory doing?

Possibly: taking pills prior to having a medically approved relationship followed, owing to a miscalculation, by infanticide, euphemistically termed abortion. Or perhaps, enjoying a "Gay" march, or maybe being brainwashed by Satan at a Rock concert. The younger victims of "state education" might be collecting unemployment benefit on account of not being able to write a literate job application letter, or they could be engaged in a riot from sheer boredom or incompatibility with their fellow "Brits" whilst their parents are battering a baby brother to death, mugging some geriatric, raping the neighbour's infant son or daughter; or more conservatively, claiming compensation for being compelled to resign from some military or police force on account of pregnancy.

Such are the products of two latest generations of State "Edjecation". The poor children are acknowledged to be released upon the world, most often in states of illiteracy and innumeracy, ignorant of their own or any other nation's history and convinced believers in evolution and the ultimate divinization mankind - or is it personkind? - - making it one with the wind or the waves or whatever natural wonder takes its fancy - no doubt the Master Race will have something to say to that.

As long as this situation persists we can never think that whatever "bit" we are doing is enough. We must double and redouble our efforts and pray for perseverance:-

To hold fast to what we have

To recover what has been lost

To unite what has been divided

To remember that who survives wins

WE DO NOT HAVE TO CONQUER THE DEVIL - JUST MAKE SURE HE DOES NOT CONQUER US.

Z

Z Z Z Z Z Z Z

THERE are people who could sleep peacefully through an anti-aircraft barrage - this writer was one of them: Remained "dead to the world" on the top floor of a convent hostel in Westminster during the "Blitz" on London in 1941, but woke up the moment the occupant of the next cubicle spoke, exhorting me to go to the shelter in the basement. I wished she had left me asleep as there was nothing one could usefully do in defence so, oblivion was best.

Now is a different story. How long are today's sleepers on the top floor going to remain unconscious under the deafening barrage of One Worldism despite all our human voices exhorting them not to descend to a shelter, but to get up and put themselves in the battle line. Who knows? One of them might be the very marksman to hit the bull's eye if he would only go to the armoury to be issued with a weapon.

If Harold Godwinson s countrymen had been as lethargic under the actuality of invasion as our supine sleepers, he would never have defeated the Danes let alone given William of Falaise and his fortune-hunting hordes such a fright. The Saxons stood on the hill at Hastings defying what looked like overwhelming odds and if all of them had obeyed their King's behest to stand their ground come what may, it would have been the Normans who would have been lost in the lake of blood at the foot of the hill the Saxons had held all day.

Gold fell the autumn leaf

Over hill and lea

When Harold pitched his camp

By the hoar apple tree.

Gold fell the evening sky

Over land and sea

When Harold fought his last

By the hoar apple tree.

Gold was the Fighting-Man.

Royal gold was he,

That fell when Harold fell

By the hoar apple tree.

We too are facing seeming overwhelming odds but, God willing, we shall not leave the hill while we live. As James Graham, First Marquis of Montrose wrote on a window pane with a diamond:

He either fears his fate too much,

Or his deserts are small,

That puts it not unto the touch,

To win or lose it all.

LAW AND DISORDER TODAY

Whenever there was or is a so-called Conservative Party in power in this country, we seem to hear or have heard so great a deal about law and order that one feels that they should be spelled with capital letters as if they were unique commodities dispensed by only the "best" stockists. It is not that the Conservatives enact more parliamentary bills on the subject than their opposite numbers when they are "In Power". Socialist governments are equally concerned with repealing Tory legislation and/or substituting as much or more of their own; all (in their case) in the cause of law and justice for all - well, perhaps not quite all - more for "The Workers" shall we say. Either way, there is an awful lot of law. We write that advisedly, for it is *really* awe inspiring what a new, improved, orderly world parliamentarians of all shades, colours and conditions are forever telling us they will achieve by passing laws calculated to regiment all lives and deaths according to the latest technological achievements, literally from sperm bank to incinerator. Perhaps not so far from the sperm in the mud as evolutionists pretend.

This legalising exercise has been the major preoccupation of politicians for so long and even more so since payment began with four hundred pounds a year - well eight months - and the right to out twist Oliver in asking for more, that one must suppose that they are motivated by some invisible authority since generations of legislators apparently never look beyond the confines of their chosen - to adapt a phrase - "House of Correction". If they had done so, and reported the results - how would they have avoided making *some* comment on the obvious and increasing chaos that obtains among the generality of those who (in this country at least) are often alluded to as the most law abiding citizens in the world. Since the dictum: "Ignorance of the law is no excuse" still holds, whilst the members of what may be termed the permanent parliament have nothing else to do but present, debate, pass or defeat bills presented by one Party or another; they must either be correcting or repealing their opponents' legislation, substituting their own, or in efforts to find occupation for idle minds, insist that some age-old vice needs to be legalised in order to give its increasingly popular performance an appearance of respectable normality. "If it is legal it can't be wrong" syndrome. Such an anomalous situation screams for recognition and remedy. However, we might say, if laws lead only to chaos, what remedy is there? There would, of course, be none, if the only Law were that which has been visited upon us in such profusion of detail for as long as most of us can now remember - but it is not. The mistake we have made, or rather, the lie that has been taught us as truth, is that law is the invention of socially responsible humanity; the crowning achievement of man evolved from primeval slime, now poised to conquer the universe. It is nothing of the kind. "Quite above our touch", as a Georgette Heyer character might say when denying acquaintanceship with some classic tome. Only the arrogance of evolutionary thought clings to the idea that "Alone we did it". But even suppose the Leaked- logic could somehow be made to hold the invention by the fitter to the fittest; it would still have to explain where those little jellies in the mud secreted the will to embark on their millennia of tortuous experimentation on the way to *Homo Sapiens*. That surely must be something of a puzzle for those who spend their paleontological lives measuring the brains of baboons.

VESSEL OF GRACE

So we shall take it that the evolutionists have it wrong. In that case, the creationists have it right, and God did fashion everything out of nothing. And He saw that it was good. So there were man and woman, created by God and privileged to walk and talk with Him in an environment of irreproachable ordered beauty. Whatever happened to that natural law and order?

One attribute God has given to man that He withheld from the animals:- free will.

With all that, our first parents had not been here for five minutes - so to speak - before they did the one thing that could send them to exile for life. By one deliberate act of rebellion they shattered forever the physical, mental and spiritual perfection they had been created with; and again relatively speaking, half an hour more and their descendants had mined the perfection of the physical world as well: their wickedness brought the Deluge down upon their heads. Ever since, nature has remained as bent as man himself so complete was his alienation from the pristine flow of Grace that only the Originator Himself could restore it. For this, The Second Person of the Triune God became man and died on the Cross to make Himself the new Vessel of Grace for the Redemption of the Fallen Race. That is the only missing link we have to discover and we have to use our free will to do it. Without Him we shall only blunder from chaos to chaos as our history shows, never more plainly than today.

Increasingly, statute books are laden with laws designed to help us to flout the Divine Will with clear consciences. Everything from blasphemy to baby murder; to natural and unnatural vice is permitted if not encouraged. Immigration and race relation laws have forced what was once a homogenous, Christian country to grant legal presentation of every other form of worship however pagan or bizarre. Legalised buggery has put our cities on a par with those of "The Plain", with even more horrific side effects than we ever learned from the bible account. Remember always: "It is in ourselves that we are underlings" Lot and his family did not want to leave the "fleshpots" of Sodom. They stayed until the very last moment, and poor, luxury-loving Mrs Lot never "made it" at all, too busy regretting "The Good Life".

The unrestrained operation of usury is really the root and trunk of this dreadful tree, since love of money fertilizes the otherwise sterile ground in which it grows. Outlaw the usurers, and the legislators will with-in law themselves and the populace be free of their now trammelling strictures.

To be effective of order, national laws must parallel the Commandments of God. As did the Common Law of England before it was dishonoured by the alien power.

However Did It Happen to Me?

by Rosine de Bounevialle.

These autobiographical writings appeared in Candour between June 1997 and August 1998. Sadly, the series was never completed.

<u>Chapter I</u>

"The Cause" I mean: I was twenty-three years old when "*we*" declared war on Germany, and only partially bemused by the Churchillian rhetoric but like most of my contemporaries, was prepared to "starve and endure". I remember saying to my mother; "Oh! How ghastly - we are going to have *years* of separation and rationing, and there will be *another* generation of 'old maids like last time'. This, on that fateful Sunday, the third of September, 1939, which shows how blind and selfish we had become since "The war to end wars" had paused at the provocative provisions of the *Treaty of Versailles*. Yet, I had no excuse for such gullibility.

I had been born and reared in what are so paradoxically called 'Roman' Catholic circles; my parents had long realised what con-trickers or ignorant tools were the majority of party politicians, and now ignored them. My father was an engineer of genius who had twice been robbed of what should have been his just return for the results of his technological expertise, which had established both his pre-and-post war employers in their "big bithnithess". The second of these cheats, he sued for compensation but lost his claim, although the defendant was alluded to in court by his own counsel, as: "My discredited witness".

After that, he determined never to be an employee again. With the willing aid and co-operation of his wife, our mother, he successfully established his family in a business property of their own - after long and ultimately successful battles with banks and local and national authorities who, as ever, did everything they could to stamp out such individual enterprise and thus prevent "escapees" from the rooted "wage-slave" society in which the vast majority clung to their "respectable" chains.

When I was eighteen, "living at home", and my brother, three years older, was employed in the Aeronautical Inspection Department with a firm in Luton, Bedfordshire, my parents, longing for life in the country turned our three storied house into as many self contained flats and found tenants for them and for the business which consisted of a petrol filling station, repair shop and twenty five lock up garages. The income from the whole enabled us to lease a modest house in Sussex. Ifield Wood, held a small eccentric community three miles from Crawley, the county capital, and there, we continued to lead a somewhat "out of this world" existence until the arrival on that peaceful scene of a septuagenarian celebrity who was known to everyone except us as the "pre-war" owner/editor of the famous and eminently controversial newspaper called *The Winning Post*, the forthright defender in libel actions brought by J.B. Joel (a South African Jewish race horse owner whose fortune derived from illicit diamond buying) and erstwhile friend of Dukes and Princes. Not surprisingly my parents thought he was a bit above "our touch" and so did not join the queue to call on him. However, curiosity (I suppose) at last made *him* call on us, when we found we were more like-minded than any others of the neighbours.

He gave us copies of his autobiography which we devoured with avidity - no wonder this man's unique contributions to the "Sport of Kings" have now been "sunk without trace" in the time dishonoured manner with which we nationalists have become familiar when studying the lives of those who have had the temerity to defy or even to disagree with the heirs of the "Hollowcost" when they are set on some course detrimental to the well-being of our *un* chosen race.

As children, my brother and I had from the age of reason, been "baby gamblers" read "racing" papers and put our sixpences (a week's pocket-money) on selected quadrupeds via "the milkman" who acted as a bookmaker's "runner" so when Bob (everyone called him "Bob") asked me if I would like to go to the races with him, I accepted with alacrity and became in very short time his "runner" and general factotum on at least four days a week in Tattersalls rings on every race course in the south of England with occasional excursions to Chester and Liverpool. So not only did I learn about horses, owners, trainers and who owned what and who was a sportsman and who was not - I understood *what* Bob was "on" about: J.B. Joel and his like were turning a sport into "bithneth" - the "big bithneth" it has since, become in which sportsmen devoted to horse owning, training and racing for the love of it find themselves pawns in a kind of equine stock exchange - well, that was the beginning, now, of course, *the industry* has gone elsewhere with all others. So Bob was almost alone in his day. He dared to wage an effective campaign against the upstarts who threatened to turn his beloved sport into the cut-throat business it has since become and *gone* to Japan, Saudi Arabia or wherever.

The result of his relentless "one man" war conducted in his own paper *The Winning Post* is, that, if today his name is known at all among members and followers in the horse-racing world, it is, infamous, as; "The man who 'pulled' Sceptre in the Derby." The Derby of 1902 that was.... the relentless power of "The Chosen" who, undoubtedly, control the means of mass communication is such that this remarkable man who achieved a once and for all quadruple success in the English Classic races and only narrowly missed making it an unbeatable record by winning all five, became traduced as a cheat who "pulled" the favourite in that now long ago Derby. The ongoing power of such defamers is only revealed when the figures and events in the classic races of those times are recalled in supposedly factual records in prestigious magazines today. "Racing" history is found to contain the same biased distortions as any other "history" when some intrepid character has incurred the displeasure of the "little lords" of money creation.

Sceptre was a "lot" in the 1900 "breakdown sale" of the then late Duke of Westminster's race horses. She was a yearling filly by *Persimmon* out of *Ornament* (own sister to the mighty *Ormonde*) which was about as high in equine aristocracy as you can get. Bob Sievier fell in love with her on sight; he was also a notable gambler - he acquired her after an unprecedented bid of 10,000 guineas (a huge amount then and almost unimaginable today!), which was scoffed at by the pundits as a case of "a fool and his winnings are soon parted." Instead, to the chagrin of the likes of jealous Joels, Sievier trained her himself at his establishment at Shrewton on Salisbury Plain and raced her with success as a two year-old. She was, of course, "entered" for all five 1902 Classic races for three year olds: ie, The Two Thousand Guineas for colts and fillies; the One Thousand Guineas for fillies only, both run within two days of each other over a mile course at the Newmarket Spring meeting. *Sceptre* won them both. She next appeared at the Summer meeting on Epsom Downs when, in those days, the Derby Trial Stakes was run over one mile and a half on the second day of the meeting, Wednesday, followed two days later (Friday) by The Oaks for fillies only, run over the same mile and a half course as in the Derby. Tragically, for Bob, she refused to accelerate after running wide round Tattenham Corner and was passed on the "run in" and finished in fourth place. In retrospect, there was no doubt in Sievier's mind that it was due to the jockey's (Randall) failure to follow his riding instructions which were to hold *Sceptre* up and make the supreme effort when "in the straight." Since she had been almost "all out" from the start and had always before been "nursed" round bends, she so resented this unprecedented treatment she gave up trying at all in "the straight". Even so she was fourth. After recovering from his speechless rage, Sievier gave Randall the benefit of the doubt as to whether he had been "bought", and put his failure to obey "instructions" down to "big race nerves". Two days later Sievier put Randall "up" again and he rode *Sceptre* as ordered when she won The Oaks with great ease.... In the Autumn, with a different jockey in the saddle she won the last 'classic' the one mile and three quarters St. Leger, run at Doncaster then, as now - when it is overshadowed by the Prix de l'Arc de Triumph. In Bob's day and until the post Second World War domination of the French over the "hostilities" starved the English racing scene, it was the ambition of every owner and/or trainer to win "the Triple Crown" (Two Thousand Guineas, Derby and St. Leger). No one, it seems, considered it feasible to expect a filly to beat the colts at the game. Surely no *sportsman* would dream of doing anything but his utmost to win, yet the slander of Sievier's perfidy was told and retold as fact from generation to generation and fifty years later in 1952, the coloured illustration on the cover of *THE BRITISH RACEHORSE* magazine for October was a mare, standing alone in a field. The identification on the "Contents" page, read:

"ILLUSTRATED COVER. The oil painting of *Sceptre* by G.D. Giles is the property of Major J. Crocker Bulteel, D.S.O., M.C., by whose kind permission it has been reproduced."

The equivalent "Illustrated covers" for the Spring, July and September issues of the same magazine each bore a coloured photograph of some celebrated horse with jockey up in owner's colours and the Contents page explanation for July read:

"ILLUSTRATED COVER. The oil painting of the Duke of 'Westminster's Flying Fox was painted in 1899 by Allen Sealy and is reproduced by kind permission of Messrs Arthur Ackerman and Son. Old Bond Street, London. *Flying Fox*, winner of the Triple Crown of 1899, was ridden by Mornington Cannon who is here depicted in the saddle against a background of Epsom racecourse, etc, etc."

One wonders why anyone in 1952 should be interested in an oil painting of *Sceptre* of seemingly no worth-while recorded history...

Well.... if *you* had paid 10,000 guineas for a yearling filly, owned and trained her for four years, run her in the five classics, backed her down to favouritism in each and won four of them, would you expect to be labelled a cheat because she failed to be first in the most hazardous of them all?

Shades of the wickedest of kings - the infanticide Richard Plantagenet!! I have told this story at length because it was the very first experience I had of the unchanging power of those that "go among them". Sievier's story also tells how one brave man can win some battles even if he cannot win the war. When Bob Sievier was sued for libel by J.B. Joel he stood in the witness box telling the truth and tossing a farthing from one hand to the other.... He was found guilty of the offence but the libelled Joel was awarded 'a farthing' damages" and on Bob's emergence from the ordeal the people outside, to the number of two thousand or so, becoming aware of the verdict followed him down Piccadilly cheering their appreciation. "The greater the truth, the greater the libel.

Chapter II

So, come 1939, and the war that was forced on Hitler, though, of course, I, at the time was as politically ignorant and duped as everyone else among "the people", but wily old Bob Sievier had smelt chicanery ever since we had all sat together listening to Edward VIII's abdication broadcast. When his forebodings were justified with the declaration and the "phoney-war" lie he said it would last even longer than the last conflict and that England would be ruined whatever the result so as he could do nothing useful for his country and the horses he loved would be "confined to barracks" so to speak, he resigned himself to die, and did so, peacefully at his home in Ifield Wood on October 8th, 1939, at the age of 78. He was "a great gun" and although we missed him very much, the confirming of his predictions during the following years made us glad that he had not had to endure them. God's mercy surely was not denied him.

By 1938 our lease of the Ifield Wood cottage (Beaumont Lodge) had run out and we had moved to an even smaller abode in Ifield Village only a mile away until my brother, on account of re-armament, was transferred from Airspeed in Luton to the same firm's establishment in Portsmouth, and our parents returned to the now vacant ground floor apartment at 94, King's Avenue, London, SW4., where the whole property (House, filling-station, lockups and repair shop) had been made the subject of a London County Council Compulsory Purchase Order, the like of which had been clamped on every property in the locality that had fifteen rooms or more situated in gardens of half-an-acre plus. All our neighbours had sold but the Bounevialle's, of course, had contested the price (4,500 pounds) determined by the Council for "94" whose then present market value was in the region of 20,000 pounds. The L.C.C. claimed that we had not had "planning permission" for the business establishment, ignoring the fact that the

Town and Country Planning Bill had yet to become an Act of Parliament at the time that the conversion was complete.

So the Council kept threatening us with THE TRIBUNAL (!) to force the acceptance of their inadequate offer and we kept saying "Yes, do let us go to The Tribunal for judgement". Stalemate.... and thus it remained "for the duration."

At the same time, the tenant of the filling-station forecourt, garages and repair shop etc: announced that he would pay only half the agreed rent, as "there would be petrol rationing." My mother still had 900 pounds to pay off the Lloyds Bank loan with which she had supplemented the cash from her aunt Miss Elizabeth Smith of Barnard Castle, which interest free loan had paid for the original adaptation of house into the silver plating business in the basement and the conversion into self-contained flats of the rest of the house. In that basement, my father operated a silverplating business, and in 1923/4 won a contract with the Canadian Pacific Railway to manufacture his own design for ashtrays to be given away as souvenirs by Canada House at the Empire Exhibition held at Wembley in 1924. The contract was for three hundred thousand ashtrays and was won against all the manufacturers in Birmingham. The proceeds paid for the development of the rest of the property except for the two year delay in obtaining the essential petrol storage licence which had been successively refused by the L.C.C., the Ministry of Health and had hovered in the Home Office until it was finally granted by the Crown Solicitors - all that about a three pump petrol filling station in Clapham Park! The two year delay was what made the nine hundred pound debt, but all would still have been short term but for the war and the tenant only paying half the rent.

So there we were, whilst the war was still "phoney", faced with receiving only half of what was an inadequate income anyway as the tenants of the flats had fled "for fear of bombs." My indomitable mother went to the bank's solicitor and asked him to serve a summons on the recalcitrant garage tenant. The solicitor told her it would be useless, as the tenant (named Packham) would certainly be judged justified in his refusal to pay more. "Nonsense", said Cis, "There is no moratorium on bank loans so there can be none on rents." So, rather sulkily, the lawyer did as she told him. When the case had been before the magistrate, we went to the bank to hear the result; a written judgement was produced which we were told permitted the tenant to remain "in situ" paying half-rent: "half-rent and mesne profits" was what the judgement said, but what we did not understand, and what the crooked lawyer did not tell us, was that the phrase meant that the tenant, Mr Packham could stay there as long as he paid the full rent ("mesne profits") plus half that sum each week until the debt was paid off. If the word had been "demesne" we might have known what the true judgement had been, but it was not and we did not, so the anomalous situation continued because naturally my mother had to agree that it would be useless to appeal.

My father, in the meanwhile had obtained a position of Inspector of Ordnance machinery in the Ministry of Supply in Woolwich and my brother had wangled his way out of his "reserved occupation" into the Royal Air Force to train as a Beaufighter pilot, first in some camp in the Midlands and afterwards in Rhodesia.

Whilst "the phoney war" continued, my mother and I stayed in the "semi-bungalow" in Hampshire, five miles from Petersfield and one from Longmore Training camp for Royal Engineers, we had occupied the place on lease since the summer of 1939.

As soon as Neville Chamberlain had made his Sunday radio announcement: "It is evil things we shall be fighting" etc: the programme for "evacuating the children" from the cities was all the thing.

My generation had been brought up in the age when most of the "middle class" had nannies, cooks, housemaids or, at least, "dailies" to do the chores, and we had had at various times, some of each kind, so to speak. Most of the "maids" came to us from the orphanage which was run on the same lines and by the same order of nuns, adjacent to one of the Convent schools I had attended from the age of six, first as a full boarder (whilst the parents were moving house) and afterwards as a "day boarder". The nuns used to help to fit these orphans for life by providing them with a good Catholic education and the equivalent of a trouseau when they became of an age to seek outside employment as apprentices or in "domestic service" if they had no aptitude for any other trade or profession. Obviously, the nuns chose what they hoped were "good Catholic homes", in which to launch their fledglings. Ours was one so we had a succession of girls of varying brains and abilities whose ambition, rather naturally was to attract some suitable male, marry and produce a family of their own. My mother was extremely popular with all of our orphans who attained such status and many of them returned for help, advice or just social visits at irregular intervals, but especially if they had problems. One in particular, having come to announce her imminent wedding, was congratulated, given a present and exhorted to "stick to the faith" as her fiancé was not a Catholic but quite amenable to: "the children being brought up as Catholics" etc. We saw no more of her until two or three years later - not sure which - she arrived one day in tears (when we still lived in London) to say that her baby was very ill with pneumonia and please would my mother come as she was afraid she might die and she was not baptized! It seemed that it was nobody's fault but Lily's, who now was hoping for a miracle! My mother said, of course the child should be baptized, and proceeded to do it with the exhortation to the erring parent that she should return to the practice of her religion and not indulge in superstition - for the child was not, in fact, dying but rapidly recovered her health, after which we heard no more of either mother or daughter until the 1940 panic stations, when we were begged by the weeping mother to accept her darling child as an "evacuee".... It was no surprise to discover that Lily was as "lapsed" as ever and her daughter who was then about eight years old was, though baptized, an innocent heathen. As soon as "invasion" was no longer expected the "evacuee" was collected and re-installed in the bosom of her family where one supposes, "the uneven tenor of her existence" was resumed.... Hope all the nuns' seeds did not fall on such stony ground.

By this time, the conscription of females looked to be certain, and as I had no desire to be "in the forces" or a "landgirl", I answered an advertisement placed by the G.P.O. (General Post Office) asking for applicants for positions requiring "slight engineering". So, off to an interview in an office in St. Paul's Churchyard vicinity in London.

After joining a short queue in a waiting room, I was ushered into "audience" where a commanding looking personage seated on what appeared to be a rostrum, gave me a page of print to read. It was of "the Cat sat on the Mat" standard. After that, another piece of paper required answers to the most elementary sums of addition, subtraction and division, which I gave. Then I was informed that the telephonists' hours were forty-eight a week and the pay fifty shillings. I said, "But wasn't there something about engineering?" Whereupon, the personage drew herself up like the caterpillar in *Alice in Wonderland* and said: "We are willing to make you a telephonist", so I crept back into my cheese and accepted.

So I was enrolled and told to report on the next Monday morning to Museum Exchange in Tottenham Court Road for Switch Board Training.

In the meanwhile, my father's youngest sister, Aunt Milly, volunteered to find me accommodation I could afford on my fifty shillings a week. She went to a Convent hostel run by the Sisters of Charity ("White Wings"), where she obtained for me a cubicle to sleep in and three meals a day for the all-in sum of twenty-four shillings a week all on the strength of my maternal grandfather, Mr Valentine Smith, "the great Catholic tenor" also known as Fabrini, the tenor with top "C". Sister Theresa, the Sister Superior was *most* impressed.

Everyone at home in Rake, Liss, Hampshire, was astounded. "What on earth are you doing?" They said: "Everyone who can is going to the country, why are you going where the bombing is'?"

My poor mother, alas, had more "evacuees". This time a family of four; father, mother and two children - or possibly the adults were the grandparents - anyway Cis (I had called her Cis since I was sixteen to break my father (Alec) and my brother, Casimir (Cas) of their suddenly acquired habit of calling my mother, "Ma-Ma"). Cis, being the sort of person she was, was very soon on the verge of starvation since she found it impossible not to share her own meagre rations with the hungry lodgers. Alec was then still in Woolwich but was later transferred to Birmingham. (Once "the second city of the Empire") in the Midlands. When he applied for the Statutory Lodging Allowance on transfer, it was refused on the grounds that he was now based there! True to form he refused to accept that.... So - Aunt Milly once more came to the rescue. She took my mother to stay with her in her rather "up market" safe suburb: Carshalton and "fed her up" (probably on the Black Market) to renewed vigour, in the meanwhile finding us accommodation in a small block of flats in Westminster within walking distance of my various places of employment in the vicinity of Whitehall, which made it possible for Cis and I to live there with (at first) the financial aid of a "lodger" recommended to us by newly acquired friend, Sophia Dragana Vanandian, of whom more later.

Alec, my obstinate parent, having failed to reach any agreement with the Ministry of Supply over lodging allowance, decided to live with us in Buckingham Gate in place of the "lodger", and travel to Birmingham every working day in order to do his job of visiting the various factories in the Midlands area to "inspect the production factories of ordinance machinery" and so fulfil his side of the contract. He did this during the remainder of "the Blitz"', travelling every weekday at 6am to Birmingham by train from London and spending the day there until six in the evening, travelling by public transport to the scheduled factories in the district, returning again to London by train, which on account of air-raid warnings might be held outside the city until the "all clear" so that my weary parent did not reach home until midnight. He did this every working day for nine months rather than submit to the cheating diktat of bureaucracy.

We had to live up to that, didn't we?

Casimir Marmaduke de Bounevialle D.F.C .

Chapter III

By 1941, we were becoming "manured" to the waste and wiles of our warmongers, but in 1940 in the Establishment induced epidemic of self-sacrifice (our sacrifice, of course, not our Directors) everything from treasured love letters, domestic cutlery, even the palings from public parks and private gardens were uprooted and handed over to "help the war effort", and doubtless, the precious, (to their owners) papers and cutlery went to join the railings in some forgotten storehouse pending the conversions that were never attempted, or intended to be so. Then, as now, however, Establishment cheats were soon overlaid by newer deceptions and so forgotten by their victims so that it was never necessary to praise or exhibit the resultant transmutations that did make me, at least, somewhat sceptical, at a later date.

In the meanwhile, my initial training for my lowly occupation was completed at Museum Exchange in Tottenham Court Road, and I was transferred to the Colonial Office, in which peaceful backwater, off Whitehall, I shared duties at the tiny (by comparison) switchboard with four other (or maybe six) staff. All of them superior, permanent Civil Servants who appeared most resentful that such a tyro should be installed in their cosy nest - and when - to my unpronounceable name, were added my amateur status, Westminster address and seemingly non-wage-earning past, my situation as the lowest ranking Hen in the Flock marked me out for anyone's pecking. Luckily, I was not there long enough for anyone to discover that I was no chicken, rather a cat, and as someone later said, where most women were stupidly catty, I was cleverly catty.... But I hope I did not scratch any innocents. In only a few weeks I was again transferred - this time, from that somewhat alien heaven to the unadulterated Hell of the Ministry of Aircraft Production - a wartime mushroom where the Ministry's telephone exchange was housed - if that is the word - in the low-ceilinged basement of a six or seven storied building on the right bank of the Thames, a few hundred yards from Trafalgar Square. The switch room had seventy "positions" ranged round three sides with supervisors' and 'enquiry' desk in the centre.

THE VERY FIRST DAY

The very first day when I entered this suffocating place, two "seniors" approached me and asked if I was a "Union" member. I said "No, I don't believe in Unions." The reply was: "Why ever not? We just got you a 'cost of living' rise." "Yes," I said, "Before that, I received two pounds ten shillings a week, after the 'cost of living' rise, which was one shilling and sixpence and put me into the Income Tax paying bracket, which tax then came to ten shillings a week, I now receive a Net income of £2-1-6 (two pounds one shilling and sixpence) instead of the two pounds ten shillings I had originally!" The Union 'reps' faded away.

There were, in those "manual" days three intolerable sins an operator should never commit - "late arrival" "excessive sick-leave" and "standing-up whilst operating the switch-board." The "chairs" provided for us were leather padded seats on steel frames, adjustable for height. After I had been employed there for two or three months - it was in 1941 - spring, I think - when one day we arrived for work to find our adjustable chairs had been replaced by small, wooden, stool-like seats with a single curved bar across the back, which were as uncomfortable as they could well be. Everyone grumbled, but no one questioned the change. After a couple of days, I said to the girl next to me, "Are you in the Union?", She replied that she was. I said "So what is the Union doing about it?" and the answer was "There's a war on, it can't be helped." Then I asked the girl on my other side and received the same replies, I stuck it for another day, and then stood up to operate. My neighbour said, "Oh, what are you doing?" I told her that I wasn't going to sit on those wretched little stools for eight hours a day. Then, my other neighbour asked the same question and got the same reply. "But," they said, "the Union say the metal is needed for the war effort." "Oh, rubbish," I exclaimed, "Don't you remember all that fuss about cutlery, park railings and even 'treasured love letters' we were all supposed to sacrifice for the war effort?' They never saw the light of day in any form, and I bet our adjustable chairs are now stored in some spare room down the corridor.".... After a few more minutes my immediate neighbours also stood up, and then *their* neighbours did the same until there were six of us in a row, all committing this heinous crime of "standing while operating!" Presently, an outraged supervisor rushed across and asked, What are you doing? I said, "We are not going to ruin our backs sitting on these non-adjustable, uncomfortable seats for hours on end." "Oh!", she cried, "They have gone for the war effort," "Nonsense," said I, "I bet they are still in the building in some store room. You only have to fetch them back." There was really nothing the embarrassed supervisor could do without taking half-a-dozen telephonists away from the 'war effort,' so we continued to operate as usual, having restful 'stands' in-between times.

The very next day, the original, adjustable, chairs were returned - even I was astonished (though I concealed it) at the rapidity of the victory. So much for Unions....

AT THE CITADEL

After five seemingly interminable months, I caught a 'flu-like cold and was on 'sick leave' when I was transferred. I do not know if the "chair" incident had anything to do with it. I rather hoped it had. Anyway, it was two weeks before I was fit to report to my next stop, which was the Admiralty in Whitehall. When I did so, I went to the main entrance and asked a passing N.O. (Naval Officer), where the Switch Room was and he said, "Oh, I'll show you or you might get lost." Everybody was supposed to have a pass complete with identity photograph, signature and all. Of course, I had not yet been issued with one which did not worry my N.O. at all - he led me by devious ways down and along into what I afterwards knew as the Citadel, (it looks something like a desert fort out of *Beau Geste*) which still stands on the corner of the Horse Guard parade ground opposite the war memorial in St. James's Park. When I arrived at the switch room door introduced by my Naval guide, two of the staff came asking who I was and how had I got there without a pass; when I told them, they cried in unison, "Oh, ! It's the Cocoa Girl." Thus Coco became my nickname. *This* switchroom was large, comparatively high-ceilinged, air-conditioned, and situated in the lowest basement of the Citadel - safe as the top brass War Room - so it was said, and by many believed, until one day, going to the canteen during an air-raid we were in a corridor of the old building and heard a rushing noise. I asked what it was, and was told "Oh, that is the air turned off from the Citadel in case there is a gas attack!" What a blessing I am not of a nervous disposition. It was still 1941. I remained stationed there until that bloody, stupid, senseless war was ended.

HOSTELITIES

It was spring and I was still living in a Sisters of Charity Hostel in Medway Street, Westminster, when the last two night-long air-raids took place. They became known afterwards as "The Wednesday" and "The Saturday". The main hostel building had five storeys but there was an annex wing which was only three storeys, my cubicle was in that, so for us the third floor was the top, where there were five cubicles, two bedrooms with doors, a bathroom, and "offices". I occupied a cubicle with a window that overlooked Medway Street and the hostel's front door, my bed was four feet away next to the partition separating me from my neighbour, the partition stopped two feet from the ceiling so that we could comfortably converse if we wished. On "the Wednesday" however, we had volunteered to fire-watch on the main building roof which was reached via a ladder from the attic on the fifth floor. Volunteers were in rather short supply because the hostel accommodated a surprising number (or it seemed a surprising number then) of girls, native to southern Ireland, who were always boasting of their brothers and cousins who were lights in the Irish Republican Army! These "enemy aliens" worked in the Registry of the War Office in Whitehall. 'Curiouser and curiouser' as Alice in Wonderland would say. Anyway, on this night, Daphne, my cubicle neighbour, and I went up the ladder to the roof at about seven o'clock clothed in a sort of female battledress and equipped with tin hats. By eight o'clock things were humming, the barrage was going full blast and bombs were falling on the City, Westminster and environs. At ten o'clock some firemen came up and told us that Westminster Hospital, which we could see a couple of streets away from our eyrie, had been hit and was in the process of evacuation; there were so many fires and wreckage that no more ambulances were available and taxis were being commandeered: on that cheerful note they departed saying, "That's right girls, stick to your posts" - so we did. A while later Daphne suddenly said, "Look! There is a man coming down on a parachute." I said, "No, it is an Earthquake bomb!" Of course we were looking in different directions - then there was a tremendous explosion on my side and I said "Your parachute man certainly made a crash landing! Then Daphne shouted, "No, look!" I turned towards her - and there sure enough there *was* a man on a parachute floating gently down - and then against all the clamorous din we both heard an ominous rushing noise like a hurricane and we both sprang for the ladder to the attic. Daphne was nearest and was on the way down - raised her head, saying "Come *on* Coco" when the thing went over our heads and seconds later there was a deafening explosion and rubble descended on us; I had my head down so the tin hat took my share but Daphne had her head up and mouth open calling me, so her lot fell on her face and down her throat but no permanent damage was done. It sounded as if the hostel had not been hit either, so we thanked

God and decided that whatever it was had not got our names on it. The battle went on and on but it seems one can get used to anything and we became almost philosophical whilst gradually the flashes and bangs, guns and aero-engine noise became more intermittent until, at last, with the dawn, there were only the dying fires and the sound of fire engines, motor and aircraft engines and slackening gunfire. We continued to wait, watch and wonder what had happened to everyone - and then we heard a voice calling rather nervously from the staircase of the fifth-floor: "Is anybody there? Are you all right?" "Yes," we shouted, "We're fine." "Oh, thank God'" said Miss Sheridan's voice (Irish but not IRA), "Sherry", we cried, "How great to hear you. Is all well?" She did not tell us at once what had made Sister Theresa, the Sister Superior, forget all about us until after 6am. Later, when we had been hailed as heroines and given the last two baths-full of hot water, (electricity supply gone) we learned that the bomb that just missed us had fallen by the front door of the hostel and wounded two of the Irish girls who had gone out during the raid, "To see the damage!" It was a major tragedy for them because, as far as we afterwards knew, they were both so badly damaged that they were never able to walk again without sticks or crutches. We saw them no more for they both remained in hospital until they were shipped back to Ireland.

I went home to Liss for the weekend and so missed "the Saturday" which saw London's last great thrashing by conventional aircraft when the railway bridge across the Thames at Westminster got its 'come-uppance' - or rather - its 'come down-ance' - but our hostel suffered no more.

ON THE FOOD FRONT

Life resumed its *un*even tenor: breakfast and dinner maintained their rationed austerity. Having been since infancy, an intermittent resident and/or scholar in a succession of Convent schools, I had long been familiar with the "Plain" Diet and uninspired cooking endemic in any establishment ruled by practioners of "Holy Poverty", so I never remarked upon it, and nor did anyone else until one day a newcomer joined our table (for six) in the hostel refectory: and this latest addition never neglected to tell the rest of us how "dreadful the food was"; as soon as the first mouthful of any meal passed her lips we were treated to this monotonous criticism. For the first couple of weeks, no one made any kind of response, thinking it would soon cease, but instead it became a sort of nightly (dis)grace until, at last, I turned to her and said, "Yes, it must be really awful for you, but for me it is a treat. You see we could only afford bread and water at home." There was a ghastly silence. The other five diners were dumbfounded - literally - thereafter, there were no more comments upon the convent's menus.

THE TINY TIGRESS

For the remainder of 1941, I was still hostel-bound, as my mother was yet at home with the "evacuees". Myself, my neighbour Daphne, and a girl two cubicles along whose name was Margaret (nicknamed Maggie-Ann) became fast friends but we had only nodding acquaintance with the other third-floorers. Then.... one evening the door of one of the end rooms (as opposed to a cubicle) burst open and a small girl (5'1") with improbable, platignum, curly hair, who resembled nothing so much as a furious tiger-kitten, erupted into the passage, saying "Ze bed, she-ees so hard!" Daphne, Maggie-Ann and I all rushed to sample the bed and greet the complaining one whom we had never seen before. We did not think the bed any harder than our own but we were fascinated by the "tiny-tigress". She had this foreign accent, Jean Harlow-like hair and was arrayed in what we afterwards recognised as a top designers' suit (it was in fact by Scaparelli!) Her name was Sophia Vanandiane but she told us that her "pet" name was Ljalja, short for Olga, Russian and pronounced "Lalya". She said she had been in Holly....hesitation...."wood" but after a few hours acquaintance, we knew there was some mystery about her - *and* surprise, surprise, she *was* provided with an extra mattress! We were all so mutually attracted that inside a week we learned nearly all about her. The reason for her initial reticence was that she had just been released from Holloway Prison - she had been fourteen months interned under the infamous 18B Order. (One could accuse anyone-else without confirming evidence, of treason and the accused might be, and often was incarcerated indefinitely without trial). These political internees were housed with ordinary convicted felons, and there was no appeal except to an "advisory council" and that, only at the Council's own discretion. This was the first any of us had heard of this outrageous extension of the First World War "Defence of the Realm Act" then known as "D.O.R.A."[22]

SOLITARY CONFINEMENT

Ljalja, was the daughter of a Russian noble woman (Princess) and an Armenian Officer in the Imperial Guard - this was reckoned a mesalliance and the despised Armenian was never promoted beyond "Captain". He was killed in W.W.1. and the princess and her baby daughter who was three years old in 1917 - escaped the Bolshevik Revolution to Yugoslavia, where the mother became a dress designer and married a Serb. Ljalja had been married - disastrously - at eighteen, to a man (Serb) who wanted no children and insisted on abortion whenever God decided otherwise. At last on her mother's advice she obtained a divorce and came to England to "begin a new

[22] Some eight hundred British men and women were held, some up to five years, because they were "fascist". Admiral Sir Barry Domville tells us in his book *From Admiral to Cabin Boy* how he and his wife were held for the whole war in separate prisons because he had been a member of a pre-war society called "The Link" which organised exchange visits between England and Germany for the purpose of healing the wounds left by the "war to end wars" and thus promoting friendship between our two peoples; mere membership was enough to warrant internment without appeal.

life" by adding English to her Serbo-Croat, French, German, Polish and native Russian languages. She went to a school staffed with Irish nuns and was accommodated more as a "paying guest" than a Sixth Form pupil. There, she became a friend of the daughter of a Rear Admiral in the Royal Navy, stationed at Portsmouth, at the time the war began, or rather was declared by Neville Chamberlain; Peggy, the daughter invited Ljalja to spend the holidays with her. They stayed, at first, in London, at the Savoy Hotel. When the Admiral and entourage were arranging to go home to Pompey, the Head Porter at the Savoy, said to Ljalja, "These are strange times, don't go to Portsmouth, go back to the convent where you are known." Ljalja, however, was, so pro-British that she had already given her binoculars and Leica camera to The Admiralty ("for the war effort"!). She did not listen to the worldly wise Head Porter's advice.... "What harm can come to me staying with my friends?" - So, she went with them to their home in the naval base. Sometime later, she was "dated" by some member of M.I.5. and when she refused the then almost inevitable invitation to fornication to round off the evening, reported her as a "dangerous spy" and she was transported to HMP Holloway where she arrived at midnight with no other explanation. She was, therefore, placed in solitary confinement pending further information. She was incarcerated thus for a whole week and treated with the utmost contempt by the patriotic wardresses - no one loves a spy - until the Governor of the prison, having received 110 further communication concerning this "dangerous spy", had her brought to his office to ask her why she was there! Her one slice of luck was that the prison was in England and the Governor humane. "If it had been in Yugoslavia", she told us, "and was also a mistake, no one would have admitted it and I would have never been heard of again. That is what made me so terrified. I thought I would be secretly murdered." So, when in answer to the Governor's enquiries, she told him her story - he believed it, and told her to send to her "friend" in Portsmouth for her clothes and jewellery which they had kept with them. Although she protested that they would be perfectly safe there, he said, "No, there could be bombing or anything; they will be much safer in the prison's lockers. At least send for your jewellery" he insisted, when she described it as valuable. So she did so, which was as well, for she never saw her clothes - or their custodians - again. It seems the Admiral had a German mistress who was the same size as his daughter's friend!

She remained in prison - Holloway - during the worst of "The Blitz" so-called, when the prisoners were supposed to be locked in their cells for the duration of "the Alert"! The Governor, however, had refused to do such an inhumane thing. This information was corroborated by another hostel guest who also had been "denounced" by a dissatisfied foreman in a munitions factory! She, however, being that sort of person, did some denouncing on her own behalf and was released in double quick time. She was English.

FREEDOM OF A SORT

After fourteen months, Ljalja at last managed to reach the Advisory Council which decided that she was innocent of spying for the enemy and could be released. So they gave her the suitcase she had arrived with, plus her jewellery, took her to the main-gate and said "You can go". "Where to?" she asked in despair: "Anywhere you like." was the reply, and the door was closed behind her. Just then a taxi drove up and disgorged the redoubtable Miss Christie. She was the Yugoslav Legation's official equivalent of a British Consul. She took her bewildered compatriot to the Convent hostel in Medway Street where she had booked her a room, explained her circumstances and informed the Sister Superior that employment had been arranged for her in the Legation; so she had been installed in the end room on our floor just the day before we met.

Everyone who had been interned, however unjustly, had their passport stamped "Enemy Alien". The appellation was never removed, so the poor girl who had been given the job of accompanying "Friendly

Alien" immigrants (Yugoslavs of dubious loyalty) to Register at Police stations was always in terror that her own credentials would be examined and her "enemy" description be uncovered. She was always telling us that she was being "followed" but we thought it was her imagination, until one day, Sister Theresa sent for us both! I was amazed to find it was not imagination, and Ljalja was horrified when Sister Theresa told us that "security" had questioned her about us both, she exclaimed "Oh, Sister, what must you think of me?" "Why" said Sister, "I said you were good, hardworking girls and no danger to anyone." She smiled benevolently upon us so that even my persecuted friend was consoled. The "Enemy Alien" tag, however, remained until she managed to change her "White Russian" nationality to Serbo-Croat some eighteen months later, when the Yugoslav Legation which we irreverently called "The Yugoslav Lunatic Asylum" turned itself into an Embassy, filled with "refugees" from the Balkans who had no inclination to join the army in the Middle East and fight for their country as their "fascist" compatriots were doing. These "refugees" were financed in their odyssey with the Yugoslav gold "saved" from the hands of both Germans and "allies" to keep the Embassy staff in luxury, first in war-torn England until they at last wore out the welcome of *our* subversive government and were packed off to Cairo, where, with hindsight we know the 'Red' brass among them were being groomed for stardom in the post war U.N. Even the "clerks" whose "war work" was to carry papers from one room to another, were paid £300 a month. What a bonanza! And not a penny to General Michailovich who remained in Yugoslavia fighting his necessarily losing battle against the Communist Tito, financed by the "allies" in which set up, Britain was the "junior partner" even then. Ljalja, did not however, have any share in the "goodies". When, at last, she asked for an increase in salary as she was so poor - she found that her wages were being paid by the Legation Councillor out of the goodness of his heart and his own pocket! Obviously, he was not "in the swim" either. To add to her terrors, the exiled Government began a correspondence with Stalin in the name of King Peter of Yugoslavia. Then, it was found that the Legation possessed no Russian typewriter, so my friend, who was the only person who could do such correspondence, had to go to the Exiled White Russian Society and use its typewriter in secret to conduct the Royal correspondence with the Soviets!! No wonder she lived in fear of every authority, and we called her place of employment - The Yugoslav Lunatic Asylum.

Rosine de Bounevialle in the 1940's

Chapter IV

By 1943, "The War" had become the normal way of life for us "reserved occupationists" and non-combatants, with "Bad News" endemic. Nightly air raids were replaced by "Flying Bombs" (V1's), the Americans came whom we enviously called "over paid, over dressed, over sexed and over here", in fact everybody came: Poles, Czechs, Yugoslavs, Canadians, Aussies, New Zealanders, etc. and so on. Our own brothers, cousins, fathers and friends of our youth were gone to the "Four Corners" as soldiers, sailors, airmen and the makers of the tools thereof. Those who were left on the mainland of Europe after the Dunkirk disaster were rounded up by the Germans and sent to their prison camps (Offlags). Stalagluft III held survivors of aircraft shot down on raids over France or on the occasional propagandist raid over Berlin. Soldiers captured at the fall of Singapore were suffering Japanese inhumanities on the Burma railway of River Kwai infame. Atlantic and Arctic convoys; abortive continental raids - news and no news were "bad news".... We ate our meagre rations and endured. Nobody thought we were going to be defeated - or if they did, they did not say so - it was just a question of: "time, and turning tides". Even the 'flying bombs" became commonplace after the initial shocks.

The worst disaster I *almost* witnessed occurred one Sunday when my mother and I had gone to eleven o'clock High Mass at the Irish Guards Chapel in Palace Street, Westminster. It was after the Offertory that we heard the distinctive engine drone of the (V1) bomb coming; the priest went on with the Mass: we were all kneeling and silent for the Consecration of the Host; at such a time, one could normally hear a pin drop but *this* day - a feather falling would have been audible. I suppose that everyone else thought as I did, if we had to die there could not be a better time or place - we bowed our heads and held our breath - I think I made a mental Act of Contrition, not sure - *and the note changed; the bomb had passed us....* The priest raised the Chalice; There was the most shattering explosion. It was as if all the Chapel windows came in and went out again but not one of them broke. We went thankfully to Communion. If we thought more about it all, we supposed it had landed in St. James' Park, but when we came out after Mass - the whole street seemed to be paved with broken glass; only then did we learn that the Guards Chapel facing the Mall had been all but destroyed during a celebratory service for some anniversary or other and the W.R.E.N's, A.T.S., Army Officers and V.I.P.'s taking part had nearly all been killed.

We went very soberly home. There was never an "incident" quite so devastating again - not anywhere near us anyway. It seems one can become "used" to anything. In summer, we underlings who worked in the offices and switch rooms in Whitehall were used to spend our "breaks" sitting in deck chairs in the park. It became quite usual when we heard a V1 coming, for everyone to look up, follow its flight until the note changed, then when the engine cut out, we turned our eyes down to the book or whatever they had been reading before. It seems very callous behaviour now but I suppose we should have gone mad if we had to imagine the consequences of *every* calamity that "did not have our names on it."

When my mother and I had been looking for somewhere to live other than St. Louise' Hostel, we had viewed five different flats or apartments, from basements to top floors, and disliked them all for one reason or another before settling in another "third / top-floor" in Chandos Court, Chapel Street, S.W. 4., where we had a "near miss"; but every single place that we had seen and rejected was destroyed in bomber raids in the following months - even the basement one! Such seeming immunity made me wonder if I had been preserved for something - especially when I thought of my experience on the hostel roof with Daphne, but from this side of memory, it looks as if I was

177

wrong - unless the deed, whatever it might be is yet to come, which seems somewhat unlikely for an octogenarian!

Anyway, back in 1943, we were still on our 6ozs of meat a week and one egg a month, when the tide had almost turned. The Eighth Army was on its way to glory, Malta was no longer besieged - my brother still survived with his Beaufighter, 227 squadron in Derna, North Africa - but the "Forgotten Army" (the 14th) still suffered in Burma; The Narvik convoys still struggled over the "Cruel Sea" whilst "Uncle Joe" Stalin clamoured for a "Second Front", "At once if not sooner".

1944: England swamped with foreigners of all colours, countries and standards - "Our Allies", a "United Nations" came to save *US* from the menacing monster over the narrow sea....

.... The ominous words "Lend-Lease" had already cast their shadow over our land. "The generosity" of our American benefactors (of which we were incessantly reminded by the traditional enemy) had rejuvenated our arms industry - or was it their arms industries? Ships, they were a building, fresh armies assembling, the bombers were smashing continental marshalling yards.... and at the same time I have now learnt, more than 50 years later, that at least, and probably many, many more than seven hundred young Americans were killed off the coast of Cornwall, England, practising beach landings, and buried secretly in mass graves, or listed as 'K.I.A.' (Killed in Action). They were rehearsing for "the Second Front" that "Uncle Joe" was so cross with us for not opening the performance of - before his slave cannon fodder ran out....?

What innocents we were, even though somewhat puzzled innocents.

The 8th Army never reached the South of France let alone Berlin. "The Allies" were suddenly "The United Nations" commanded by one Eisenhower, a pet, we later learned of the, also suddenly significant: Bernard Baruch, (advisor to no less than *five* Presidents of the United

States). Such a favourite was this "pet" that he had been elevated over *three hundred* more senior and capable officers, to become the Commander-in-Chief of the invading force, of the aforesaid "United Nations" *and* the stooge participant in some of the most hideous of war-and-post-war crimes that (one hopes) will ever be committed - (No, *not* the hollowcaust) - for these he was rewarded with The Presidency of the United States of America, whilst his partner (junior), Winston Spencer Churchill, (another protégé of Bernie's) whose part in those *un*publicised, charnalhouse, **real** holocausts made "The Greatest Living Englishman"....may God Help him - also responsible for:

The devastation of the undefended cities of defeated Germany.

The starvation of herds of helpless prisoners, German, (See the Morgantau Plan!)

The Atomic Destruction of Nagasaki / Hiroshima when Japan was suing for peace.

The triumphant vengeance of the self-chosen-Talmudic-race-of-Jews on *every* Christian Race and Nation. Those Jews who made themselves the limbs of Satan in his and their pursuance of their Devilish Destiny since the fall of Lucifer and the "Chosen Ones" repudiation of their true Messiah, Jesus Christ, in favour of today's clamour for their ONE WORLD of mongrelised slaves ruled by the *Devil's OWN*.

It is only NOW that I realise that the code name for the "Second Front" was not selected at random

OPERATION **OVERLORD**

Shades of Bernie Baruch....

Rosine de Bounevialle - A Life in Pictures

Rosine with her family in 1917

Rosine with her brother Casimir in 1918

Rosine in fancy dress c. 1933

Rosine in the 1930's

Casimir and Rosine pictured c. 1940

Rosine as drawn from a photograph, 1946

In Jersey at a L.E.L. meeting in 1958

Disguised as an Indian Empire Loyalist at the Albert Hall, 1958

Electioneering in 1964

In South Africa, late 1980's

With Romanian guests at Forest House, 1995

With Colin Todd, 1990's

Rosine in July 1997

About The A.K. Chesterton Trust

The A.K. Chesterton Trust was formed by Colin Todd and the late Miss. Rosine de Bounevialle in January 1996 to succeed and continue the work of the now defunct Candour Publishing Co.

The objects of the Trust are stated as follows:

"To promote and expound the principles of A.K. Chesterton which are defined as being to demonstrate the power of, and to combat the power of International Finance, and to promote the National Sovereignty of the British World."

Our aims include:

- *Maintaining and expanding the range of material relevant to A.K. Chesterton and his associates throughout his life.*

- *To preserve and keep in-print important works on British Nationalism in order to educate the current generation of our people.*

- *The maintenance and recovery of the sovereign independence of the British Peoples throughout the world.*

- *The strengthening of the spiritual and material bonds between the British Peoples throughout the world.*

- *The resurgence at home and abroad of the British spirit.*

We will raise funds by way of merchandising and donations.

We ask that our friends make provision for *The A.K. Chesterton Trust* in their will.

The A.K. Chesterton Trust has a **duty** to keep *Candour* in the ring and punching.

CANDOUR: To defend national sovereignty against the menace of international finance.

CANDOUR: To serve as a link between Britons all over the world in protest against the surrender of their world heritage.

Subscribe to Candour

CANDOUR SUBSCRIPTION RATES FOR 10 ISSUES.

U.K. £30.00
Europe 50 Euros.
Rest of the World £45.00.
USA $60.00.

All Airmail. Cheques and Postal Orders, £'s Sterling only, made payable to *The A.K. Chesterton Trust*. (Others, please send cash by **secure post**, $ bills or Euro notes.)

Payment by Paypal is available. Please see our website **www.candour.org.uk** for more information.

Candour Back Issues

Back issues are available. 1953 to the present.

Please request our back issue catalogue by sending your name and address with two 1st class stamps to:

The A.K. Chesterton Trust, BM Candour, London, WC1N 3XX, UK

Alternatively, see our website at **www.candour.org.uk** where you can order a growing selection on-line.

The A.K. Chesterton Trust Reprint Series

1. Creed of a Fascist Revolutionary & Why I Left Mosley - A.K. Chesterton.

2. The Menace of World Government & Britain's Graveyard - A.K. Chesterton.

3. What You Should Know About The United Nations - The League of Empire Loyalists.

4. The Menace of the Money-Power - A.K. Chesterton.

5. The Case for Economic Nationalism - John Tyndall.

6. Sound the Alarm! - A.K. Chesterton.

7. Six Principles of British Nationalism - John Tyndall.

8. B.B.C. - A National Menace - A.K. Chesterton.

9. Stand by the Empire - A.K. Chesterton.

10. Tomorrow. A Plan for the British Future - A.K. Chesterton.

11. The British Constitution and the Corruption of Parliament - Ben Greene.

12. Very High Finance & Policy of a Patriot - Paul Cahill & Otto Strasser

Other Titles from *The A.K. Chesterton Trust*

Leopard Valley - A.K. Chesterton.

Juma The Great - A.K. Chesterton.

The New Unhappy Lords - A.K. Chesterton.

Facing The Abyss - A.K. Chesterton.

The History of the League of Empire Loyalists - McNeile & Black

The Sound the Alarm Collection - A.K. Chesterton.

All the above titles are available from The A.K. Chesterton Trust, BM Candour, London, WC1N 3XX, UK. (www.candour.org.uk)